3/14

AMERICAN HONOR KILLINGS

AMERICAN HONOR KILLINGS

DESIRE AND RAGE AMONG MEN

BY DAVID McCONNELL

Published by Akashic Books
©2013 David McConnell

ISBN-13: 978-1-61775-132-5
Library of Congress Control Number: 2012939273

All rights reserved
First printing

Akashic Books
PO Box 1456
New York, NY 10009
info@akashicbooks.com
www.akashicbooks.com

for Edmund White

TABLE OF CONTENTS

Author's Note

Readers may want to know a thing or two about how I researched and wrote this book. Events in some of the early sections had already been extensively reported long ago. Recasting facts using literary techniques—imagination excepted—is an illuminating process central to this work (I don't think a writer's sentences and "the facts" are really two different things at all), but it would be wrong to pass off somebody else's investigative work as my own. So I've tried to be clear when I lean heavily on another person's research. This is notable with the series of *Sacramento Bee* articles on the Williams brothers' case, most of them by Sam Stanton and Gary Delsohn, as well as with an essay the pair wrote for *Salon*. It's also true for an ABC News *20/20* broadcast and a *Frontline* documentary, both on the murder of Billy Jack Gaither. My brief account of the Schmitz/Amedure case relies entirely on very widespread newspaper reporting at the time and on the former Court TV's coverage of subsequent trials. I had issues of interpretation, and even fact, with all of these reports (and many more), but it wouldn't be right not to disclose that the major news-gathering work had been done before I came along. That said, I wouldn't have included the stories unless I had something new and substantial to add beyond my words and sentences.

More recent events didn't get nearly as much attention. Though I still read everything I could, I had to collect most of the information myself. Except for places in Northern California and Idaho connected with the Williams case, I've visited every significant locale mentioned in the book. Every quotation and every other detail is accurate to the best of my knowledge. Whenever I've speculated at obscure moments in the narrative, I've been clear about it.

Occasionally, when a sense of inner life seemed necessary, if only for the sake of basic understanding, I also allowed myself some clearly identified speculation. Otherwise, whenever someone "thinks" or "feels," it's because they later stated that they did, usually to me.

Sources are listed extensively, by name when possible, in the acknowledgments at the end of the book. Anyone curious to see a small sample of the material I used in my research can go to americanhonorkillings.com, or to my website, davidmcconnell. com, where I have posted, along with commentary, a dossier of photographs, links, and documents to accompany each chapter.

1
INTRODUCTION:
SPECIES AND REALITY

As a child I could hardly master my terror of a particular encyclopedia page, a tipped-in color plate illustrating species of bees and wasps. I knew exactly where the page came in the book, and as I neared it, my eyes squinted half-shut and my leafing hand moved more and more slowly. The page—this was a very old encyclopedia—was covered by yellowed glassine paper, but that only made the images, which showed through dully, more horrifying. Pictures and reality didn't feel safely different enough to me. A fear that intense is also fascination, so I kept going back to the book pretending that I wasn't deliberately risking my fingertips with those monstrous insects.

Working on this book has involved a similar fascination and aversion. There's lurid and uncomfortable content, yet I've felt compelled to learn and tell as much as possible. I'd like to think I've been as precise and informative as a natural history illustrator, though my subject isn't as well defined as bees. It's men and their anxiety and violence.

As I researched and wrote, it dawned on me that you can't talk about violence among men honestly without also talking about sex. The fact is, all relationships between men—friendship, rivalry . . . murder—are casually characterized by sexual metaphors. Everybody's familiar with the sexual nature of male vulgarities, trash talk, locker room boasting. We see the obvious link to competition, violence, and aggression, but we don't want to think deeply about what the sexual words actually mean.

A man I know from a rough masculine milieu happened to invite a gay friend to dinner with his buddies. Afterward, he commented to his friend in wonder, "I had no idea we talked so much about gay stuff." Only self-consciousness about the presence of a gay friend had made it apparent to him.

I had a similar epiphany while writing this book. By picking situations where straight and gay men came together and the result was conflict and murder, I realized I'd hit on a "trick" to observe a mostly unspoken truth about violence and men. The metaphorical and the real neatly aligned.

I worry a little about aversion on the part of some readers, and not just to the difficult subject matter. I've written a story about men. Around half of them, most of the victims, are gay. Many people still find it hard to accept that gay men are part of the story of masculinity, but they are, and understanding what goes on in this book demands an integrated view of men. There are different—many—kinds of men, but none belongs to a separate species.

That said, the modern gay demimonde looms large in a few places, so this particular story of men could only have taken place in America or in another developed Western country. But once again, as I worked I felt the story burgeon under my typing fingers with almost chemical energy and I understood that the fundamental subject is ancient. This isn't a discussion of one decade's or even one century's mores.

To cover as many aspects of the story as I could, I've taken a handful of American murders and retold them in narrative form. The telling is simple. Interpretation is kept to a minimum. The language is frank and sometimes offensive. The stories are all more or less recent, but together they make for a little study of things unspoken until now. I've deliberately looked at different parts of the country and different subcultures. The actual sexuality of the players is surprisingly various, and the motive for murder is different in every case. Picking stories that were all alike could have turned into a political or forensic exercise. I wanted to conjure reality. My approach was literary, not academic.

I haven't treated straight men with quite the respectful delicacy they may not even realize they still expect. A common American image of men as rough, clumsy buffoons is probably the product of the powerless fondly teasing the powerful. Another—men as terrifying brutes—may come from the powerless raging against the powerful. But straight men, who really are socially powerful, have been accustomed to a veil of discretion when it comes to the truth about their private selves, their weaknesses, anatomy, fears, silliness. Beneath the cartoon images of men, a profound discretion is still largely intact. In some cultures, image alone—an exaggerated, feline dignity—defines masculinity itself. Because masculine notions of honor and privacy and dignity play such a huge role in the story I tell, I had to be careful I didn't subscribe to those notions myself. You can't leave it as an unexamined truth that men are a certain way if you're trying to write about how they really are.

As cold-eyed as I've been about the sensitivities of straight men, I've been just as cool to the myth-making of gay activists. The gay people in this book, unlike those in a politically aware Hollywood movie, don't instructively embody the exact opposite of every gay stereotype. One or two appear to have tawdry or uncomfortably stereotypical lives that would make sophisticated straight guys blanch, not at the homosexuality—who cares?—but at the cliché!

"Hate crimes" and "gay panic defense" are terms used by activists and lawyers. They weren't what interested me, though they were my jumping-off point. (After all, these were situations where vastly different sorts of men came together.) I wanted to write something humane but politically indifferent. I settled on the exotic-sounding words "honor killings" in the book title because, incredibly, that's what these crimes resemble. America isn't organized by clan or tribe or even family. It's a nation of individuals and groups based on culture or identity. The seat of honor for men is personal, religious, racial. And among the worst affronts to that honor today are gay sexuality, "immodesty," and "decadence." These killers weren't outraged because someone made a pass at them. They saw, or needed to see, themselves as believers, soldiers, avengers, purifiers, as exemplars of manhood.

What emerged as the prime mover of violence in these cases was a shadowy and explosive tension I invariably observed in the minds of young men, something I'd experienced myself. It begins, I suppose, as self-consciousness about one's own masculinity. It can involve a fear of being unmanly, or a fear of being *seen to be* unmanly. It can be a fear of being or being seen to be gay. It can be the weight of religious or cultural beliefs about behavior hammered into you or the simple, spooky realization that without those beliefs or social inhibitions nothing *really* prevents you from being, for example, a coward or having sex with another man. The tension can even be a rage at feeling self-conscious about these things at all. Sometimes tension devolves into an ecstatic contempt for social pollution or for what young men, hungry to take their place in the world, see as social pollution—an assault on the traditions they've just learned (the forensic psychologist Karen Franklin has pointed this out). It can be an intoxicated hatred for and need to separate oneself from a weak or inferior class of people. Anyone can experience this miasma of thought. It's familiar to some women and to many gay people. But straight or gay, it's the special province of young men, especially when violence comes into it.

Yet I don't want to insist on ignoring gay and straight. A look at the short history of the scorned "gay panic defense" gives background to the story. Claiming gay panic is the legal strategy used to describe the kind of violence I had in mind when I started my work, the kind that occurs when different types of men come into conflict. The story goes like this: A pervert hits on a nice American boy who reacts with shock and outrage. Understandably, things get violent, and the pervert winds up dead.

The popular idea that only repressed homosexuals can really feel gay panic is false. But that was the original idea. The term "homosexual panic" is usually traced to a 1920 article in the journal *Psychopathology*. The author, Edward J. Kempf, was writing about soldiers he'd treated who experienced a paralyzing conflict between homosexual desire and heterosexual expectations. But the Kempf cases don't have much to do with the legal invention "gay panic defense," which is recent.

Though it's likely defense lawyers engaged in ugly hinting to juries long before then, the first explicit "gay panic defense" occurred during *People v. Rodriguez* in California in 1967, not coincidentally just at the media dawn of "gay liberation." Rodriguez was running wild with friends, one of whom had just snatched a purse. When an older man came into an alley to see what was up, Rodriguez threatened and beat him with a branch. The man died. Belatedly, Rodriguez claimed he'd been urinating. The man, he said, came up behind him and started touching him or reached for his penis. The jury didn't believe it.

A handful of cases followed in the '70s (e.g., *People v. Parisie* in 1972, *State v. Thornton* in 1975, *Commonwealth v. Shelley* in 1978). But the "gay panic defense" only entered popular consciousness with the so-called "Jenny Jones" murder in 1995 and with a cluster of cases in 1998–99, including the most notorious of all, the murder of Matthew Shepard (though in the Shepard trial the judge refused to allow a gay panic–like argument).

Looked at legally, there's a very narrow historical window for a crime of exactly this type. Gay panic couldn't exist before "gay" was perceived as a separate condition, a shift in outlook historians often locate in the late nineteenth century (though that's extremely contentious). Since then, a young man could—in theory—panic because he was taken for "homosexual" rather than because he feared seduction or rape or insult. But the historical window seems to be closing fast. Gay panic crimes can't occur except when being gay is perceived as so horrible that it induces understandable panic. Judges and juries are increasingly unlikely to understand the reaction themselves or to tolerate it in others.

If the legal "gay panic defense" has an expiration date

that's passed or approaching, at least in the United States, the experience it purports to describe may be dying out, as well. Gay isn't quite the big deal it used to be. We don't nod in comprehension when anger is a young man's automatic response to another man's desire. At least the more sophisticated among us don't. But, again, this isn't one decade's story. The deeper subject of the book wells up. If I struck "gay" from this book, or miraculously made "gay" a social and cultural nonissue with a wave of my hand, almost nothing I've written would change. I've written about young men and pretense, pride, tension, fear, arrogance, ignorance, anger, foolishness.

In a sense the story begins with the *end* of gay panic. The murders in this book don't look much like that kind of crime. They're far more complicated, atavistic. Hence, "honor killings." They involve honor, manhood, desire. When used in the phrase "honor killings," honor obviously has a negative connotation. We're not talking about real honor. But remember, the nineteenth-century campaign against duelling also involved a conceptual attack on the meaning of honor. With the very modern imagery or reality of sex thrown in, these crimes are the remote cousins of duels.

Of the cases I studied, only one looked anything like an authentic instance of gay panic. That was the "Jenny Jones" case in 1995. Jonathan Schmitz, a troubled young man who'd already attempted suicide twice, was pestered by the attentions of a gay man, Scott Amedure. The "pestering" was the kind of thing considered cute in romantic comedies, but as women know, cute masculine movie behavior doesn't transfer well into real life. Amedure and a friend tricked Schmitz into appearing on the *Jenny Jones*

Show. During the show Amedure revealed his secret crush on Schmitz. Though for a couple of days Schmitz tried to absorb what he felt was a huge public embarrassment, he eventually snapped. You could say he panicked. He killed Amedure with a shotgun and promptly called 911 and confessed.

Interest in the Jenny Jones case ran so high, so much was written about it, so many Court TV broadcasts devoted to it, that the story acquired a false air of familiarity. This is common with our headlong news media. Each new detail or development in a story is prefaced by a recap of what's already happened, which becomes ever briefer and more formulaic. When I looked at this story I did nothing more than assemble the details into a simple narrative for my own convenience. The result was completely unexpected.

In news accounts, the painful story was lost in moral grousing about trash TV. And, as always in these cases, the rumor started that Schmitz had to be gay himself. He wasn't. In fact, he'd made some effort to be relaxed about the gay issue with several gay friends and with Amedure himself, but his good looks and perhaps his palpable vulnerability made him an object of sexual fascination for both men and women. The issue for him was a deformed idea of personal honor. I've written Schmitz twice to ask for his opinion about my take on the case. He hasn't replied.

At the Chicago studios of the *Jenny Jones Show*, producer Karen Campbell and associate producer Ron Muccianti conducted preshow interviews on a Sunday morning. They were skilled at shepherding wide-eyed guests through the hectic routines of television.

Shortly after arriving, Jonathan Schmitz accepted

a beer to take the edge off his nerves. As if no time had passed since the phone call months before inviting him to go on a show about "secret admirers" (apparently he had one), the young man again tried to get Karen to tell him what to expect. He said he didn't want it to be a guy. Karen later testified that she told him it could be a girl, a guy, or a dog. "I told him, *It'll been fine, Jon. Relax. Have fun. Someone likes you.*"

Jon, as everyone called him, was pint-sized and cartoonishly handsome in his brand-new collarless shirt. Slightly prim, bee-stung lips set on a broad, Kennedyesque jaw cried out for caricature. His eyebrows were black-as-greasepaint circumflexes. The out-of-fashion way he feathered his dark hair couldn't undermine overall classic good looks. The eyes, best of all, were startlingly pale green. Like a movie star's.

Later, Jon's father Allyn pulled a heavy curtain across his son's childhood, saying only that he was a "normal kid" until he started having problems at eighteen. The problems were drinking, depression, anger. Because mental illness so often starts in adolescence, the problems may have been written, or at least outlined, in his genes. Jon's maternal grandmother was manic-depressive. In 1988, Jon had to be hospitalized for a week for depression. He was diagnosed with bipolar disorder. He'd attempted suicide quite recently, after his girlfriend Kristen broke up with him.

Those working on the show had no idea how fragile Jon was. After speaking with him, Karen Campbell went to talk to the secret admirer himself, who was waiting in another room. Scott Amedure seemed wired, curious about everything. ("Is this a green room?") His face was flushed. After an easy chat (getting Scott to half-rehearse what he'd say on air without realizing it was rehearsal), Karen jotted down a note for Jenny Jones: *Scott has an inkling that Jon is bisexual. Jon's going to die when he sees Scott!* She folded the note and had someone take it to the star.

In yet another room, Scott's "gal pal" Donna Riley, who was going to appear on the show with him and who had originally introduced him to Jon back home in Michigan, was being interviewed by Ron Muccianti. An open bottle of Absolut vodka and tumblers were on the table. It was unclear whether the vodka was there to help guests relax or to loosen them up. No one said anything about it, Donna later remarked. It was just there.

Ron Muccianti reportedly asked her, "You had the feeling Jon was interested?"

"We think he's a little gay at least," Donna said.

When he appears on the clip I saw, Scott is grinning so hard his cheeks must have been sore. The audience hollers. He wears a dark vest. His thinning hair is slicked too flat on top. He's pale-skinned, seems prone to flush, and is near-enough blond that the mustache he's trying to grow has a juvenile transparency. His troublemaker's smile and trim, jittery good looks are the "bad boyfriend" kind some people adore. (A friend later recalled that Scott always got whatever guy he went after.)

He's a born performer. With show-offy bashfulness he seems delighted by the crowd's enthusiasm about his crush. Everybody roots for a lover. He describes his first meeting with Jon: "Saw this little body sticking out from under her car." Jon had offered to do some work on his neighbor Donna's car in the parking lot of the Manitou Lane Apartments where they both lived. After meeting Jon from the neck down, Scott's crush developed quickly in the succeeding days. He found a chance to leave a friendship bracelet for Jon at Donna's apartment. It was never picked up. Jon said he was straight, but Scott was undaunted. A flier Scott found in a gay bar (*Same sex—secret crush?*) inspired his *Jenny Jones Show* ploy.

Only once, after Jon agreed to appear on the show and was getting excited about it—getting his hopes way up that the admirer might be his ex-girlfriend Kristen—did a sudden, clear-headed premonition cause him to question Donna and Scott. He wanted to make sure Scott wasn't his secret admirer. No, Scott and Donna said, they didn't know anything about it.

On the show, in spite of all the encouragement, Scott sounds a touch reluctant when he's prompted to repeat the fantasy he must have rehearsed minutes before with Karen Campbell. "I'd like to tie him up in a hammock." The audience laughs warmly and starts applauding again. Scott takes a countrified gulp for breath, glances at the star, and plunges on: "And it involved champagne and whipped cream and stuff like that . . ." He grins. Loud applause. He must have been feeling invincible. He glances at Donna in the chair next to him, huge in a garish red sweater. She hunches her shoulders and holds her tiny hands in her lap. Her smile lingers stiffly as her gaze skitters over the audience.

Jenny Jones seems to glow. The TV lights raise a resplendent aura from her oversprayed blond hair. Her creamy, condoning WASPiness makes her seem the perfect patroness for lowlifes. There's nothing teasing or superior in the gentle, half-apologetic way she gestures across the stage with her microphone and colored note cards. "Jon?" Jon comes out.

He looks at Scott and Donna sitting there. All smiles. He walks toward them saying through his own smile, "You guys lied to me," while the audience howls.

Scott moves to hug Jon. They embrace briefly as if with spring-loaded arms. The noise is incredible. It goes on and on, even after Jon sits down. He can't suppress a smile. His hands rise and neatly cover his face. The smile reappears as soon as his palms hit his thighs again.

Jon functions affably enough. He grins the way we do when we've been had. In a small, unadorned voice he informs Jenny, "I'm definitely heterosexual."

With a jocular flicker of grousing, Scott tells her, "Well, maybe he'll be less nervous around me now."

After the show, producer Karen Campbell says, she asked Jon whether he'd be all right flying home on the same plane with Donna and Scott. He told her he was okay with that. Of course, the show must already have bought three tickets on the same flight, but now there was no need for discussion. Jon seemed fine.

Although Jon downed another beer after the show, it had no apparent effect. He must have been brooding within. The show's three Michigan guests weren't seated together on the plane. Jon appeared nervous to the woman next to him. Perhaps because she was wearing a friendly expression, Jon explained apropos of nothing, "I had a weird day." The woman introduced herself as Pat—Patricia Cielinski.

Jon told her about the show. Pat understood that he'd been ambushed and later testified that he told her, "What if my grandparents or my parents think I'm really that way? I didn't do anything to make this happen." He told Pat he'd spent six hundred dollars on new clothes for the show. He mentioned that he'd been hoping the secret admirer was his ex-girlfriend Kristen and that he'd considered proposing to her on air.

More mildly, Jon concluded, "I'm not angry. But I'm sure if I sit down and think about it, I could get really mad."

The strange Sunday went on, unspooling in an emotional tangle. After the plane arrived in Detroit, Jon offered to drive Donna and Scott back home. Perhaps it felt like the gentlemanly thing to do, in spite of everything. Yet somehow the three decided to stop for a drink together. They went to Brewski's, a chalet-style roadhouse. Two gigantic wooden eagles carved with a chain saw supported a gable over the entrance. The companions ordered a pitcher. They were having a nice time as far as their waitress could tell. Jon sat on Donna's side of the table. She later testified that at a certain moment he threw his arm around her and nuzzled her shoulder.

After Brewski's, Jon drove the other two back to the Manitou Lane Apartments. When he pulled in he hit a guardrail and smashed his right front headlight. Scott and Donna invited Jon up to Donna's for a nightcap. Like an automaton he followed. All three sat around in murmurous quiet for who knows how long, then Jon said goodbye.

After Jon left, Scott mentioned that Ron Muccianti had told him the broadcast (which was never aired) was planned for "sweeps week." He told Donna she'd better warn Jon. But the two friends had to have been deeply confused by Jon's contradictory behavior. It occurred to Donna at Brewski's that maybe Jon was interested in a three-way. As if nothing had happened, Scott started spinning anew his fantasy of hooking up with Jon. He told Donna that he was going to ask Jon to go with him to pick out a ceiling fan for his vinyl-clad trailer in Orion Parks. The two would install it together. Scott slept on Donna's couch that night.

The next day, Monday, Scott probably felt a slight letdown because the wild ride in Chicago and on the show was over. He called friends and told them everything in detail. He called his mother, Pat Graves, who wanted to know how Jon had reacted. She later claimed Scott told her that he and Jon had had sex after the show. She insisted on this until her death. It's easy to imagine a misunderstanding, or subtle fib, if Scott put it to her like this: "Hell, I spent the whole night with the guy last night." But as she remembered it, Scott told her, "We spent the night together. I'd say that pretty much tells you his reaction."

Recounting the story to his mom and friends apparently wasn't enough for Scott. He called Ron Muccianti next. When he told Ron that he'd "spent the night" with Jon, Ron shouted out to the people in his Chicago office, "I think we got a love connection, guys!" To Scott, Ron dangled the possibility of a follow-up show—Jon and Scott together.

Meanwhile, Jon got into work late that Monday. He looked disheveled. "Who was it?" was the big question at Fox & Hounds, the restaurant where he worked as a waiter. He told his boss, "I'm not mad yet." During lulls, he played a game of pool and a game of darts with coworkers.

On Monday night he called his father Allyn. He started sobbing. He was drunk.

Allyn got pieces of the story out of him like pulling boots from mud, and became alarmed. He knew how dangerous it was when Jon descended to these abyssal lows.

Jon told him about "wrecking" his car, complained about the cost of repair, and insisted that he hadn't asked for any of this.

Afterward, Allyn called his daughter, Jennifer Yoakum, and asked her to look in on Jon when she got a chance. Undoubtedly, both were dreading another possible suicide attempt. Like the first time with Allyn's own heart medication. Or the second time with different pills. Or like the terrifying time Jon bought a shotgun. A few days later he returned it for two hundred dollars, still unopened. Allyn told Jennifer he didn't think things were that serious but that Jon had had a bad time on the show and was drinking again.

The next morning, Tuesday, March 8, Allyn stopped by the Manitou Lane Apartments on his way to work. He found his son distraught. Awkwardly, Allyn tried to comfort Jon. He says he told him that even if Jon really were gay . . .

Jon was late again to Fox & Hounds. Asked whether he was mad about the show, Jon told a coworker that he'd trashed his apartment the night before. A waitress, Michelle Wright, was worried about him. At the end of their shift, when she was pulling out of the parking lot, she saw Jon's small, dark figure come out of the restaurant. She testified that she flashed her headlights at him to get his attention and invited him over to her place for a drink. Jon accepted.

Michelle lived with her parents, so she and Jon had to be especially quiet. They shared a drink or a joint. Michelle says she let Jon sleep on the couch.

Maybe Jon was disoriented when he woke up on Wednesday morning in sweat-softened clothes. Maybe it took him a moment to recall where he was. Remembering Michelle, the show, the world, and Scott probably came over him like a leaden wave. He was out of Michelle's house by about nine a.m. and back at his own place at the Manitou Lane Apartments by ten.

An amber traffic warning light sat flashing silently in front of his door. Yellow "crime scene" tape zigzagged over the door. No one was around, but Jon probably felt exposed and embarrassed as if the Jenny Jones millions were watching. He pulled open a note taped to the door. *John. If you want it "off" you'll have to ask me. P.S. It takes a special tool. Guess who?*

Ironically, Scott had misspelled Jon's name.

Jon shut up his apartment, drove off, and withdrew $340 from a drive-through cash machine. It was a little after ten. He then went to Gary's Guns and asked the clerk, Nancy Morgan, for a twelve-gauge pump-action shotgun. $249. As he filled out the purchase form with perfect self-control, he mentioned he was planning to do some hunting. He drove to a second store, Tom's Hardware, to buy shells, a box of five hunting loads. He knew plenty about guns from his childhood in small towns in Minnesota and Indiana, before the family moved to Michigan.

He drove back to the Manitou Lane Apartments, where he opened the shotgun package and assembled the weapon, toylike with its plastic stock and rubberized recoil pad. New guns have a clean-seeming oiliness, like a film of sweat. It was still only ten thirty when he pulled out again.

At Orion Lakes, Jon left the shotgun in the car. Scott's roommate, Gary Brady, answered the door of the trailer. For a second the two must have looked at one another uncomprehendingly. Jon knew nothing about Scott's roommate.

When this cute, serious stranger asked for Scott, Gary let him in. After Scott came out, Gary left the room so the two could be alone.

There must have been some exchange about the note Scott had left on Jon's door. Whatever was said was brief. Jon returned to the car.

Gary stuck his head in when he heard the door close. "What was that all about?" Scott waved him away. Gary realized Jon was coming back. He withdrew again and waited in a bedroom. He listened.

The screen made a twang. As Jon entered, he chambered a shell with the big mechanical jerk you use with a pump shotgun.

Scott may have seen the barrel as Jon entered and tried to press the door closed again. He fell back. "Gary, help! He's gotta gun! He's gonna shoot!" Scott grabbed a wicker chair, holding it up to fend off Jon.

Jon fired through the chair into Scott's chest. Gary came into the room. In disbelief, he watched that cute, calm boy from a moment before rack the gun and chamber a second round. Noise and motion of some kind were coming from Scott on the floor. The blasted chair had tumbled aside. Jon fired again.

Hysterical, Gary called 911. His call came in at 10:58 a.m. Jon had gone. After the call, Gary says, he remembers hearing the amazingly loud hissing-spattering sound of air escaping Scott's lungs through the wounds in his chest.

Jon stopped at a service station and called 911 from a pay phone. He wept when he explained to the female operator what had happened. He mixed little boy's diction with the words of an angry man: "He picked on me on national TV. He fucked me." The operator kept him talking until a police cruiser pulled up. Cautiously, a patrolman approached the man on the phone. Reddened eyes shifted to him, tears streaming. "The gun's in the car . . . I just shot somebody."

The long legal aftermath of the "Jenny Jones" case was continuing in 1998 when Matthew Shepard was murdered. His story immediately became emblematic of this kind of crime. An enormous amount has been said about that case, which is persistently murky, but at the time gay people were galvanized. Shepard's mother wrote a book and became a potent political force in her own right. The country was entering an era of "hate crimes" which appears to be continuing. A black man, James Byrd Jr., had been killed that summer in a grotesque racist attack. And four months after Shepard's Wyoming murder, Billy Jack Gaither, a closeted gay man, was killed in Alabama. The story I have to tell next happened during the summer of the same year, 1999.

The Williams brothers didn't commit an individual murder but made a bizarre attempt to start a holy war in North Central California. The mayhem culminated in the killing of two gay men. The double murder was purely ideological. Nothing in the least sexual ever transpired between the murderers and the victims. In fact, the sexual issue comes up only obliquely as the story proceeds, along with racism and anti-Semitism. But it's appropriate to start with a wide shot of America's religious and cultural landscape of intolerance, the habitat of a certain dark, masculine ideal. If Jonathan Schmitz felt his personal honor needed defending, here we have the fantasy of a whole culture in need of defense against decadence. This type of violence is often "inspired" policing or a maddened drive to purify society, as Karen Franklin found. The Williams story offers a portrait of a young man as a deluded kind of savior.

2

MATSON, MOWDER, AND THE
WILLIAMS BROTHERS, 1999

I. An Education

California's Tennessee-sized Central Valley doesn't feel like the California of TV. Its northern end, the flat, well-tended Sacramento Valley, breaks into dreamlike oceanic hills that crest around Sutter Buttes, a huge volcanic island right at the center of the valley. Fields of trained kiwi fruit vines look exactly like vineyards. This farm country has an earnest middle-American beauty with a hint of Southern Europe thrown in.

On hot days the silence is so deep that a soft, unnameable swish can be heard in the background. It seems to come from all sides and fill the world. It's a boring, ominous noise like a snake's one-note crooning, impossible yet oddly familiar.

Here, opposite a peach orchard on Higgins Avenue, behind a listing white picket fence, a house is nestled among trees and organic garden plots. As neighbors recall, every so often a tall man in a sun hat strode off the property. Turning right toward Myers Avenue, he walked and preached to the world. He carried a staff like Charlton Heston's Moses. Otherwise, he was dressed in jeans and boots like any boutique walnut or kiwifruit farmer from around here— Gridley, California. He didn't seem completely crazy. An unpleasant, almost-aware-of-it smile sometimes formed in the white thatch of his half-grown beard. But you didn't want to get caught on the listening end of his harangue. He'd park his gaze stubbornly on the sky or on the dusty margins of the road. He'd take a deep breath and continue his sermon right at you. Nothing as hackneyed as *Repent, for the end is nigh!* But neighbors suspected that was the gist of it.

Ben Williams may have been unlikeable but probably wasn't dangerous. His wife Sally, ten or fifteen years younger, seemed laid-back, kindly, a touch fluttery, and not in the least overawed by her husband. She taught elementary school down in Yuba City. People said Ben had once worked for the US Forest Service, but now he simply ruled his one-acre Eden on Higgins Avenue. And occasionally preached like this to no one or everyone.

As Edens have to be, the place was cut off from the world. Planting screened the house from the road. Sally left to go to work, of course, but the family kept to themselves. Between the vegetable patches and berry bushes, chickens for laying and for slaughter, little needed to be brought in. As far as possible, the modern world was kept out. To Ben and Sally, even the conservatism of Reagan's '80s couldn't disguise an America in full decline. Their two boys were homeschooled.

Some neighbors shook their heads when the older boy got it into his head to start preaching like his father. Matt was dark-haired, pretty, preternaturally self-possessed. He paced around spouting what sounded like Bible verses in a wild soprano. The stolid younger boy, Tyler, sometimes trailed him, and the family dog, Shadow, an Australian shepherd, sometimes shadowed Tyler. It was weird, but maybe it wasn't *that* weird. They were enthusiastic about their religion. So what? Kids have to make their own fun in farm country.

Matt and Tyler seemed too odd to be popular with other children. In any event, their parents disapproved of contact with most outsiders. (Sally's sweet expression could flutter into one of surprising toughness.) People from church were safest. Tyler sometimes joined kids a few doors down for a game of basketball. But on the whole life revolved around home studies, work in the huge garden, and services at whatever evangelical church the family attended at the moment. Though Ben threw himself into church life with near-incoherent passion, he was liable to break with a given pastor at the drop of a hat. The family would switch to a new church, until the next irresolvable conflict came up.

When they got older, the boys started going into Gridley to attend high school. Ben didn't want them involved in school activities, so they came home as soon as classes ended. The social incommunicado was harder on Tyler than it was on Matt. Unlike his older brother, Tyler may not have had the imagination to participate in the family's shared inner life of virulent religiosity, thrilling symbolic intuitions, and nightmarish political insights. Matt, on the other hand, flourished on Higgins Avenue. He was growing up the image of his father.

Neither parent was happy when Matt graduated high school and announced he was ready to go out on his own. But they couldn't isolate him from the world his whole life. Matt joined the Navy and, after "nuke school" (shipboard nuclear power plant training) in Florida, he was stationed in Bremerton, Washington, across Puget Sound from Seattle.

On base Matt was considered strange. His mom's indulgence probably meant he'd never had to regulate his intense enthusiasms. He could seem prissy about some things. Then again, he always sat too close. He forever touched arms and shoulders and backs. Out of the blue he'd say something fond about you right to your face. How could you respond to that? He just didn't have a regular guy's taut self-repression.

To American sailors in 1990, Matt's behavior didn't call to mind "homeschooled, isolated, doted-on." It called to mind "gay." A friend later said he got fed up always having to mutter, "Dude, back off. Gimme some room here." So one day this friend asked what he and the others had been thinking. Was Matt gay or what? Matt was stunned. How could anybody *ever* think he was gay? He couldn't leave it alone. He came back to it for months. "Why would you think that about me?"

Matt had a couple of things going for him. His unedited enthusiasms made for real charisma. Plus, in a gun-toting culture his easy relationship with firearms, especially his pet Glock 9mm handgun, earned him respect. His gun savvy had come from his father who'd often dismayed the neighbors on Higgins Avenue by standing on the porch to take potshots at starlings or scrub jays attacking his plums.

During this time a friend, Todd Bethel, took lurching videos of the California boy: Matt misfiring and frowning at the Glock somewhere in Olympic National Park, Matt in a room mugging gangsta-style with a fan of hundred-dollar bills cashed from his sailor's paycheck. It looks for all the world like he was trying to become a regular guy.

And yet, Matt may have been feeling a subterranean tension. For him, the messy, painful conflicts of adolescence had never happened. He believed as firmly as ever that his father was right: those who walked with the Lord, the truly virtuous, were a besieged and minuscule band. The Navy and Bremerton were providing his first true glimpse of the immensity of the corrupted world out there. Raised on prayers, epistles, psalms, and gospel, the rolling rhetoric of scripture was very likely the language of Matt's thinking.

After Thanksgiving, Matt put in for early discharge. Perhaps he was feeling the pull of family and Gridley. But just as he was about to leave, he met Kimberly Rogers at church. She was evangelical too. She found him irresistible.

To look at, you'd have assumed Matt was cocky or unpleasantly suave, but his awkward energy could charm. He was TV handsome, almost too refined-looking for Bremerton, like an admiral's son incognito in the swarm of oafish, jug-eared sailors. Fine dark eyebrows crossing a wide forehead, fine nose, fine red mouth on an elfin chin, fine ankles, fine wrists, fine spiritual fingers, his body had been whittled down to the elegant essential.

Matt talked, Kimberly listened, they dated. Just like that, she was pregnant. Of course, she was going to have the baby. She wasn't a murderer. But Matt's intensity had started to make her uneasy. Already he made all the decisions. Her first real decision was not to marry him.

Many things suggest Matt was shocked by her refusal. It wasn't just the sin. His shock must have been personal, like the appalled disbelief an artist feels when the work of a lifetime is shrugged off by critics. Kimberly was rejecting the masterpiece of the Gridley workshop—himself. His friends report that he was shaken—but they probably couldn't guess the extent of it.

Things got worse. A little girl was born. Matt wasn't

about to keep this from his parents. Disappointing them must have crushed and terrified him.

On a personal website Sally reported with leathery cheerfulness that at exactly this time, the fall of 1991, "a time of personal crises," she took up watercolors. She describes herself as forever at the easel singing "praise songs to Jesus/Yahshua" while she painted. Until recently the website still displayed and offered for sale her many paintings. She did a vase of red tulips that later won a prize. She painted crystalline views of Sutter Buttes in the distance. Selling a few of these pictures must have been a consolation. The family had never had much money. But her chief aim in painting, according to the website, was to glorify Yahweh. She's been described to me around this time wearing a broad-brimmed hat and linen skirt and looking almost like an old-fashioned hippie. But she was a contradictory, Pauline sort of "hippie," whose website would later quote the epistle to the Philippians, "whatever things are lovely . . . think on these things."

After a couple of years at home, Matt left California a second time in 1993. He was twenty-five. He was going to try to jump-start his life by finishing college. He enrolled at the University of Idaho in Moscow, declaring a major in biology.

Moscow and its twin college town, Pullman, Washington, six miles due west, are in the Palouse, a vast prairie and one of the world's most important wheat-producing regions. The hills of the Palouse look like one of Grant Wood's surreal farmscapes. People say the Palus Indians, cousins of the Nez Perce, gave their name to the prairie, but an apt confusion with the French word for "lawn," *pelouse*, might have been involved too.

Besides being farm country, a better fit for Matt than Bremerton, the Palouse had something else he may or may not have been aware of. For historical and geographical reasons, eastern Washington, northern Idaho, and western Montana are probably the whitest, most Christian part of the United States. The area is sometimes imagined as part of "Cascadia," a fantasy all-Caucasian nation, by racist dreamers. Barring occasional bloodshed—the shoot-out at Ruby Ridge, for example—residents roll their eyes at the area's tax protesters, racists, and UN-phobes. But in a conservative, deeply private, deeply religious region, madness and tolerated eccentricity can be hard to tell apart.

Matt Williams had been in Moscow only a few days and knew no one when he was approached by a team of kids from the cultlike Living Faith Fellowship. They introduced themselves with, I imagine, the hard-smiling friendliness that looks so false to skeptics like me. Matt, however, responded with enthusiasm. He joined up. Like his father, he was both driven to and despaired of belonging. In the Living Faith Fellowship he thought he'd found the perfect home away from home.

As part of church indoctrination, Matt was interviewed in depth, encouraged to confess his sins and failings. He later said he told them about his ruined relationship with Kimberly and about his illegitimate daughter. This information would have been entered on a standardized form. His photograph would have been paper-clipped to his file. Like most church members Matt wasn't told anything about the church files.

Mistrustful of the outside world, the church involved itself in the private lives of its members, especially in their relationships and marriages. Associate pastors didn't hesi-

tate to suggest or discourage matches. Ex-members complain they were often berated and kept in a fog of self-doubt.

The church had a policy of protecting its flock from
dangerous books. Members submitted to church leaders
any books they intended to read. Though the process might
take months, the book was vetted and either approved or
rejected, perhaps with an inquisitorial, *Why would you want
to read this?* Bizarrely, Matt felt right at home in an atmosphere others have described as a nightmare of manipulation.

In the fall of 1994, a group of disaffected Living Faith
members began meeting, often at the home of Jeff and
Ann Monroe in Pullman. To this day Jeff and Ann share
an easy friendship unusual in couples. I interviewed them
together, and their banter is charming. Back in the day
both struggled to diet, yet forgave themselves for being
overweight. They preferred focusing their energy on others. They agreed that something had to be done about the
bewildered young people lured into Living Faith.

Jeff and Ann's group started posting warnings about
the church on bulletin boards at university campuses. By
winter a full-fledged battle for student sympathies was un-
derway and made it into the local papers.

Cult or not, Living Faith reacted to the negative public-
ity like a simple-minded tyranny. The church dispatched
shock troops of student-believers to rip down fliers at all
hours. A flier freshly stapled to corkboard at, say, two in
the morning vanished within an hour.

Matt Williams in particular threw himself into the defense of Living Faith. He later said how much he'd loved
the quasi-military midnight campus patrols. For him, the
strongest and best beliefs involved action. But it seemed
the strength of a belief meant more to Matt than its con-

tent, because in two weeks he switched sides, won over by a book (*Churches That Abuse*) and by a Christmastime meeting at Jeff and Ann's house. He went from tearing fliers down as a good soldier of the Lord to putting them up with equal joy as a fiery partisan of the truth.

Once Matt left Living Faith he needed a new object for his wild devotion, and he focused on Jeff and Ann. They were charmed and taken aback. It was as if a hyperarticulate puppy had entered their lives. Matt started calling the Pullman couple his spiritual father and mother (as the leaders of Living Faith had been called). He asked advice on every aspect of his life: work, love, belief. Jeff became "Pastor Jeff." Some days, Jeff told me, he was sure it was all just playful admiration, a flirty, childlike bid for affection. Then Matt would bow his head and soberly confess that he hoped Jeff would find him a wife, and Jeff realized that, incredibly, this wasn't a game. Or was it that nothing separated play and earnestness in Matt's mind?

Matt's open-hearted sensitivity could be eerie, like the time he called Jeff following a party to ask after a person he thought had seemed unhappy. He gave friends poems, thoughtful presents like Christmas ornaments of little mice in calico, cookies. He placated the whole world the way a brilliant little boy will placate a doting mother when she's sad or distracted. His generosity was all the more impressive because he was the poorest person Jeff knew. Matt was living on about a hundred dollars per month, including his seventy-five-dollar-a-month rental at a Moscow trailer park.

But Matt caused problems too—puppylike problems of too much enthusiasm, or so it seemed at first. Matt was now anti–Living Faith with a vengeance. Others in

Jeff and Ann's circle were unnerved by his intensity. His with-us-or-against-us absolutism made him a divisive figure. A crazy suggestion to assassinate church leaders was just—crazy.

More disturbing still, a girl Matt dated briefly confided in Jeff that her relationship with him had been miserable. It wasn't only churches that abuse. Matt had been like a one-man, domestic Living Faith Fellowship. He'd immediately established complete control over the girl's time, activities, and thoughts. Even as he railed against the church, he seemed oblivious to his own manipulative behavior. And he was erratic. Sweet, haranguing, apologetic, hysterically funny, cruel, in moody syncopation. It was scary.

After hearing from the girlfriend, Jeff was horrified. He'd introduced Matt to another girl he knew. Now he regretted it. Now he understood why the date hadn't even lasted the whole evening. Yet Matt claimed to long for a simple, Christian married life. He sometimes talked about it in a way that made Jeff feel a sense of pity. Dream and likelihood were worlds apart.

As it had with the sailors in Bremerton, it did cross Jeff's mind that maybe Matt was struggling with his sexuality. There was the time Matt—very hesitantly—said that he'd gone hiking naked with a friend. He asked whether Jeff thought that was gay. Matt got the awkward question out in his docile, what-should-I-do voice, and "Pastor Jeff" tried reassuring him. To Jeff, Matt's physical ebullience—his frequent hugging, for example—ultimately seemed more infantile than closeted. The pressing issue for Matt was acting human, not acting heterosexual. And nakedness by itself wasn't at all unusual for him. He was, in an exuberant, Edenic way, a naturist.

Physical perfection—purity—besotted Matt. He left pots of tap water sitting so the fluoride would settle out. After abruptly turning vegetarian, he became adept at "food combining," a faddish, complicated nutritional system meant to ensure perfect health. He came to believe drinking so-called "colloidal silver" could boost his immunity, perfusing his body with naturally antibiotic silver particles. Jeff and Ann had some old silver-plated cutlery. Matt got battery, wires, silver spoon, and alligator clips arranged in a circuit and started brewing the omnipotent silver ion solution. From there, he went on to kombucha tea. Soon everyone in Jeff's circle seemed to have a bucket of the stuff fermenting under their sink. The kombucha "mother" was a brownish mat of bacteria and yeast growing on the surface of the tea. With the unsqueamish tenderness of the true gardener, Matt would peel a layer from the living "mother" whenever he wanted to get a new batch going.

Around this time Matt self-published a forty-eight-page booklet entitled *Optimum Health and Longevity*. In the breathless voice of crackpot religious pamphlets, he condemns caffeine and television. He explains that AIDS can be transmitted in saliva and aerosols. Not so puppylike suddenly, he inscribed a copy to Jeff and Ann, *May you continue to shed those evil chains. The perverters of truth shall die.*

Matt's fads didn't just involve health and nutrition. Those were the easiest to talk about. His greatest intellectual thrills were ideological. He flirted with the fundamentalist King James Only movement after reading about it online (the movement maintains the King James translation of the Bible was divinely inspired). In the spring of '95, Matt got hold of a book that sparked a political craze for tax avoidance. The book, by Lynne Meredith (now in federal prison for conspiracy to defraud the IRS), claims the government has no constitutional right to collect taxes. It's written in a style Matt favored, an expository crazy-quilt of typefaces and quotations.

Matt started trolling the Internet daily and debating a fellow student, Karney Hatch. Hatch told me Matt would argue with an ever-reappearing smile and constant eye contact. He backed up his points with lightning biblical citations. Of course, what the Bible said proved nothing to Karney, raised an atheist, and even Matt seemed to understand that his fundamental argument—which was an argument from faith, after all—had to emanate hypnotically from his eyes, his lips, the peace of his expression, from the unstoppable music of his words, as much as from their meaning.

Most of Matt's friends describe his years in Moscow as a decline into extremism. In his spiky handwriting (he was forever writing letters, journals, pamphlets), Matt once wrote Jeff Monroe, "I engaged three Mormons (actively) in 'combat' the other day. They are jumping onto the Ecumenical (bowel) movement . . ." As a fundamentalist Christian, Matt considered Mormonism beyond the pale. Here he's mocking the Mormon willingness to engage with other faiths. But he writes, and thinks, in conceptual curlicues. His sentences become a chopped salad of capitalizations, parentheses, and ironic quotation marks. The sentence quoted above breaks off with a long dash, so he can address Jeff directly: "—shift gears: It is nice to have friendships (rare) in which the members of such can speak into each other's life via exhortation."

It's hard not to frown at the revealing strangeness of

Matt's wording there. Isn't "exhortation" how you speak to a crowd or a flock, not a friend? And isn't speaking "into" another's life a lot less intimate than just speaking "to" a friend? It sounds lonely.

The small trailer park where Matt was living was just off the University of Idaho campus, across South Main (State Highway 95) from the Business Tech building. As he spent more and more time at the trailer, junk accumulated on a porch addition he'd built. Matt had some heated exchanges with his landlord, who thought the place was starting to look trashy. (Like his father, Matt was touchy about his rights.) An avid recycler, Matt had gathered shards of a broken mirror. He fitted them into an esoteric design on the outer wall of the porch. The design was a crowned sword with an extrawide "N" for a hilt, a *Wolfsangel* turned on its side. When Jeff visited he recognized this as a symbol of the "Christian Identity" movement. It explained a troubling reference Matt had made to "mud people" when talking about African American football players.

Jeff was becoming increasingly worried about his friend. Printouts of bizarre Internet articles were stacked three feet high in the trailer. A weird steplike block of wood sat in front of the toilet. Matt had learned to draw the Hebrew tetragrammaton ("YHWH," in English letters, it's read as "Yahweh" or "Jehovah"). He hung versions of it all over the walls. Money was a bigger problem than ever. He'd sold his CDs. His friends had pulled back.

In 1995 Matt saw the Mel Gibson movie *Braveheart*. The macho kitsch of *Braveheart* has a quasi-pheromonal effect on many young men of Matt's stripe. After seeing it, he felt compelled to bike all the way to Pullman to talk to Jeff and Ann about the movie—and his life. He came in, sat

on the couch, and spoke to them in a semicoherent mono-
logue that made Jeff and Ann feel they might as well have
been house cats. Rehashing Gibson's story of masochistic
self-sacrifice, of masculine honor, Matt worked himself
into such a state of yearning ambition that he broke into
sobs several times. When he abruptly got up to leave, Jeff
and Ann were so stunned they didn't know what to say to
stop him. Or if they wanted to. (*Braveheart* foreshadows in
a glorified form some of the later events of Matt's life. It's
hard not to imagine that Matt often thought he was living
this silly dream of manliness and insurrection. The movie,
which won five Academy Awards, has a crudely propagan-
distic antihomosexual story line.)

When his brother Tyler made an extended visit to Moscow, Matt went into a manipulative frenzy. Jeff and Ann
describe a weary and shell-shocked younger brother, an
ever-inadequate member of Matt's personal Living Faith
Fellowship. In a thickening mist of fatality, Tyler probably
couldn't grasp the tyranny he lived under at his brother's
trailer. He had to read the books Matt told him to read. After getting out of the shower one time Tyler shut the bathroom door. Hypervigilant, Matt demanded to know why.
Tyler answered that he needed to take a dump, of course.
Through the thin trailer wall Matt then told Tyler exactly
how to do that. Naked astride the little toilet, Tyler obe-
diently lifted his feet to that strange block of wood. Only
when you raise your feet, Matt explained through the wall,
is your spine curved enough to ensure a proper, natural
bowel movement. You should always do it that way. Feet
on the block, knees raised, Tyler's gut tensed as ordered.

Tyler told Jeff and Ann this story. They repeated it to
me. It sounds like madness. Who needs to be in charge of

the way another person takes a shit? According to Jeff the story came out sounding flat and sad. Worse, unaccountable tears welled up in Tyler's eyes. The way Jeff and Ann smiled and held themselves with house-of-cards breathlessness may only have made the moment worse.

Somehow Matt had gotten into Christian Identity ideology. That mirror mosaic sword is its symbol. Amid the tangle of beliefs we avoid thinking about when we lump together skinheads, neo-Nazis, antiabortion madmen, racialist theorizers, right-wing Christian cultists, and all their kind, Christian Identity has, at least, a better story than most. Adherents tend to use the "correct" names "Yahweh" for "Lord" and "Yahshua" for "Jesus." They feel an affinity for Hebraisms partly because Identity's central, dumbfounding belief is that the Israelites, the Ten Tribes, the people biblical prophecy is about, the "Chosen People," are not the Jews but the "Germanic, Nordic, Celtic, Anglo-Saxon, Danish, and allied races"—in other words, Aryans. Everything is backward. Conventional biblical history is a case of mistaken identity.

Some prolix Identity types retail tedious magical scholarship to prove that modern Jews are descended from the "Khazars" of "Khazaria," a kingdom thriving between the Volga and the Don (or in Gog and Magog) during a shadowy stretch of the first millennium. But for many the story begins at the beginning.

God created the "beasts of the field." That accounts for "mud people"—all people of color. They're not human beings and have no souls. The history of real people begins in the Garden of Eden. Just after Adam inseminated Eve, Satan came to her in angelic form and inseminated her again. The Adamic seed produced Abel; the satanic seed, Cain. Satan, through Cain, is the forefather of the Jews. The Jews escaped destruction during the flood and have been waging a bitter war on humanity ever since. They've almost won. The imminent apocalypse will begin with a racial holy war because the Messiah can't return until the world is cleansed of abomination.

Identity's "Church Fathers" in the United States are Wesley Swift (1913–1970), Nord Davis Jr. (1931–1997), Ted Weiland, and Pete Peters (who now abjures the term "Identity"). Randy Weaver of Ruby Ridge believed in or had some loose connection to Identity. (Loose connections are usually all you get in a subculture of messy-minded loners.) Identity's star turn came as the "state religion" of Richard Butler's Aryan Nations (their flag bore that crowned sword and *Wolfsangel* cross, and they were among the first to propose an all-white homeland in the Pacific Northwest, the so-called "Northwest Territorial Imperative"). Allies of Butler helped form "The Order," the group that assassinated Alan Berg in Denver on June 18, 1984. Believers in Identity may be more prone to violence than other racist and religious nuts, because they see themselves as an "Eleventh Hour Remnant" of the Chosen People. Their holy war is always just beginning.

It's tempting to laugh at that Garden of Eden story. Like most extremists, Identity types are often more clownish than scary. A large measure of their dignity is reflected back on them by the alarmists and self-important law-enforcement officials whose careers depend on an enemy. Still, it's sobering to imagine Identity from the inside.

For many of us, Adam, Eve, and Satan carry no more emotional punch than Astarte or Baal. Most of us have only

encountered anti-Semitism as a fading middle-class vice.
To a believer in Christian Identity things look different.
You're out in farm country. Everything is slow. You're full
to bursting with language, but the world is mute except for
that uncanny snakesong. The truth comes to you with a little jerk of certainty. You've never met any Jews, but they're
everywhere in the Bible, history, and the news. How have
they managed to be uniquely persistent, as every other
nation fell and every other race mongrelized? They even
look—the pure-bred ones—like Satan: the nose, the dark
eyes, the mercantile grin.[1] Why is so much always made of
the Holocaust? Why is the United States such a toady for
Israel? Why is the worst American cultural sin anti-Semitism?
It all makes sense if the far-off metropolises of the world
are controlled by a multimillennial secret society, a partially satanic race.

Those cities are in chaos. Children are regularly stran-
gled, dismembered, and vacuumed from the wombs of
ignorant girls. Race traitors interbreed with soulless mud
people. Drugs, filth, and abomination are embraced by
urban orgiasts. You've never met a self-proclaimed homosexual, but it's obvious homosexuality has nothing to do
with desire, certainly no desire a normal person could feel.
Homosexuality is "Gay." It's a big-city cult of makeup, dis-
graceful clothing, lasciviousness, lisping sarcasm, and decadence. Its goal is an end to generations, an end to history.
It's the preeminent invention of the Jews, a cult of steril-
ity and death. This universal city—Pandemonium—is the
enemy of a tiny, rural, outgunned, outwitted, *Braveheart*-like
band of yeomen Christians. It all makes sense: you're at war.

---

1. Of course, in truth, it's Satan who, historically and quite deliberately, looks a little
like a Jew.

II. *The War*

Early in 1997, the Williams family moved to a larger property an hour and a half from Gridley in Palo Cedro, east of Redding. Palo Cedro and Redding are at the far northern end of the Sacramento Valley, where the terrain begins rising toward the high country around Mount Shasta. But the property really wasn't so different from Gridley. The new house was on Oriole Lane and backed up on Cow Creek. The family set about recreating Eden.

Over several years, neighbors watched the property slowly disappear as new planting came in. Ben tended golden delicious apple trees. Sally later wrote on her website that "her son" (my instinct says Matthew) planted a pineapple quince especially for her. She did a painting of it. A bed of black hollyhocks was put in where she could see and paint them from her window. As they had in Gridley, the family raised ducks and chickens. Banties were a favorite, because, again according to Sally's website, she liked their colorful, flowerlike plumage and fierce motherly instincts.

During his first years in Redding, Matthew becomes hard to pin down. On the surface, there's not much to tell. He worked at a nursery briefly. Then he and Tyler started a gardening and lawn care business. Tyler was living on Oriole Lane with Ben and Sally, but Matthew took an apartment in a motellike complex on the 1900 block of Hartnell Avenue in Redding, ten or fifteen minutes away. He joined the Redding Certified Farmer's Market and set up a booth there on market days. It was a natural extension of work he'd done in Idaho at the Moscow Food Co-op. The people who met him found him unfailingly polite—"nice, educated, smart . . . quiet, mild-mannered," one market acquaintance was later quoted in a newspaper story. He enjoyed sharing his considerable knowledge of botany and horticulture.

But something more was going on in Matthew's life. In January or February of '98, he was spotted selling literature in the lobby of a Redding hall where Militia of Montana founder John Trochmann was giving a speech. Trochmann, a bald man with the dandified white beard and glare of a Confederate cavalry officer, was then traveling the country giving lectures about Y2K (remember, the dreaded year-2000 computer apocalypse?). When the organizer of the event, Larry Wampler, was later phoned by a *Los Angeles Times* reporter and asked how well he knew Matthew Williams, he said, "I had no influence on him. John Trochmann had no influence on him." (Wampler suddenly interrupted the interview, saying, "The FBI is at the door.") Though they may not have known him any better than the farmer's market crowd, Matthew obviously had connections with the political fringe.

In April of that year, a *Redding Record Searchlight* columnist got a letter from a reader bemoaning the "folly" of integration. It came from Matthew. He wrote that strength through diversity "is a great lie that should be obvious to anyone observing modern America." He wrote another letter to the founder of the National Alliance, William Pierce, author of the notorious race-war saga *The Turner Diaries*. A draft of that letter was later found by the FBI.

Matthew hadn't fallen completely out of touch with his old friends from the Palouse. They got letters too, disturbing ones. "Dearly beloved, I have just finished the most exciting and relevant Bible Study of my life! A special person shared IT with me and I want to share IT with the special people of my life . . . I reckon that thee shall be blessed by this greatly." He mentions Pete Peters, Ted Weiland, and Nord Davis Jr. by name. He even praises the infamous, zombielike Okhrana forgery, *The Protocols of the Learned Elders of Zion*. He suggests his friends arm themselves in preparation for imminent unrest. You can almost sense his excitement about this fantasy. The widely reported nervousness over Y2K can only have made his millennial emotional knowledge feel more certain.

In December, Matt tried to reach that college friend, Dan Martin, who'd gone with him on the naked hike back in Idaho. A mutual friend told Matthew that Dan had finally left the Living Faith Fellowship and begun a new life. "He came out." Dan Martin was now working with the Stonewall Health Project in Moscow. He'd found a circle of gay friends. Matthew responded as if Dan had been in a car accident. He reportedly cried.

Just before his family moved to Redding, Matt would also have learned that Kimberly Rogers, the girl he'd asked to marry him, the mother of his daughter, had finally married another man. Maybe that, or his thirtieth birthday in 1998 or the news about Dan Martin, helped precipitate what happened next. But all three events could just as easily have been irrelevant to someone like Matt who was immersed in faith and a growing sense of mission. Jeff Monroe told me he sensed that Matt had given up on normal life, perhaps on life altogether, even before he left the Palouse. Yet he was still dreaming. Three months before the crimes, he wrote Jeff a letter mentioning a new girlfriend in Colorado. Matt called her "my Rocky Mountain lass."

It was 1999. For most people the millennium was an enjoyable curiosity. Maybe it meant something, maybe it didn't. Certainly, it gave a boost to the "Preparedness Movement," those who awaited some kind of social or natural calamity. Preparedness was the term of choice, because by now everyone knew "survivalists" were bunker-happy kooks. Preparedness was a natural for Matthew, though it could have been more than just a timely fad. (The buyer of the old Williams house in Gridley reported that for years he received all kinds of survivalist literature addressed to the former occupant.)

In Matthew's case, at any rate, the calamity was going to be RaHoWa, in-the-know shorthand for "Racial Holy War" (and the name of a popular Canadian white supremacist band with two discs issued by Resistance Records).[2]

On February 19, Matthew drove down to Sacramento to attend a "Preparedness Expo" at the Cal Expo state fairgrounds. In later interviews he would point to this visit as the start of everything. Hoping to meet like-minded people he clipped a small sign to his backpack: *The White Race, the Earth's Most Endangered Species*. The "endangered species" tag line is something of a trademark for the National Alliance, the flagship white separatist organization at the time (the one founded by William Pierce, who wrote *The Turner Diaries* and to whom Matthew had addressed a letter). It's a best seller for them on all kinds of merchandise.

Matthew had a good chance of finding a brother in be-

---

2. There've been a lot of racist bands, part of a fertile white supremacist youth culture. Matthew probably knew RaHoWa, the band. He quotes a Nine Inch Nails song and *Atlas Shrugged* by Ayn Rand in a letter sent from prison. On the same page he writes, "RaHowA [sic]/its [sic] a battle cry/RaHowA/its do or die/RaHowA/our spirit shall never die/RaHowA/its a saintly cry!" That sounds like the misremembered lyrics of RaHoWa's song "RaHoWa" from their 1995 album *Cult of the Holy War*: "Rahowa!/It's our battle cry. You're trembling in fear/cause of this look in my eyes, Rahowa!/It's the white man's call,/ You can chase me to the end of the earth,/but I shall never fall, never fall . . ."

lief at Cal Expo. Years later, online, I discovered a short memoir of that year's expo by a man who'd moderated a panel. The man describes ex-sheriff and right-wing activist Richard Mack responding "to the critics of 'right-wing conservative wackos' who accuse us of racism and bigotry. He called to the stage . . . an Hispanic woman, a black woman, a native American man, a pacific islander man, and a Jewish woman." On the same panel Joseph Farrah "addressed the morass of the mainstream media"; Terry Reed, author of the underground CIA exposé *Compromised*, talked about Clinton corruption; Bo Gritz burned a small UN flag, his usual stunt; and Dr. Len Horowitz spoke about the dangers of AIDS, Ebola, and "emerging viruses." The panel moderator waxed enthusiastic on his blog, "The people I met and saw covered a wide spectrum of society. From the guy who makes his own Colloidal Silver to the guy who bought a nineteen-thousand-dollar item at a charity auction . . . from the mother of a pilot concerned about anthrax vaccines, to the man moving his family to avoid the worst case scenario of Y2K. They were all different, yet all the same." There's no knowing whether Matthew attended this panel, but it's tempting to imagine he's the one described as making his own colloidal silver.

Matthew says he met someone at the Preparedness Expo. The person noticed the sign on his backpack and invited him to join an unidentified organization. His new friend explained that initiates had to take part in a group activity. Matthew says that four months later he and eight other guys from south Sacramento (no one exchanged names) met at a strip mall in the capital city at around two a.m. Homemade firebombs were passed out.

There's reason to believe Matthew made this story

up. Whether he really had underground connections is a good question, though. He knew Larry Wampler, at least in passing, and his background makes it look like he could have been either a joiner or a loner at this stage. But even if he did meet someone at Cal Expo in February, no shadowy organization invited him on a secret mission. That isn't to say he hadn't started thinking about a mission himself, about action, about resurrecting the thrill of his midnight campus sorties for the Living Faith Fellowship.

The movie *The Matrix* opened on the last day of March 1999. A drawing Matthew made in prison and entitled "The Destruction of the Magog MATRIX" contains imagery suggesting he saw the movie. The nothing-is-as-it-appears-to-be paranoia, the Christlike central character, and the gorgeous violence all would have been intensely appealing to Matthew watching from his own looking-glass world.

A month later, it begins. April 20 was Adolph Hitler's birthday. Anti-Semitic fliers were found at four high schools around Redding, California. Unknown at the time—Matthew and Tyler Williams did the leafleting. No one could remember anything like it happening before. The episode got shocked local news coverage.

Meanwhile, Hitler's other birthday remembrance that year eclipsed this provincial case of nasty leafleting. Eric Harris and Dylan Klebold shot up Columbine High School on the same day. The Hitler's-birthday connection kept being talked about after the Colorado school massacre. As was the killers' decision to wear trench coats, which some thought was inspired by costumes in *The Matrix*. It's worth imagining what went through Matthew's mind as he watched, heard, or read about this: there were others like him out there. He was part of something larger. This really could be the beginning of the Apocalypse in America.[3]

While he was following news coverage of Columbine in May and June, Matthew was making war plans. He started on the Internet. It's easy to find recipes for home-made incendiaries online, from a sugar/potassium chlorate mixture to rough-and-ready napalm made from gasoline and Styrofoam or gasoline and dishwashing liquid. Matthew opted for a straightforward accelerant, a two-to-one mixture of gasoline and oil. He and Tyler filled one-gallon black plastic jugs of Mobil Delvac 1300 Super with the mixture. They used up most of a case of the motor oil. They did the work at their parents' Palo Cedro property in a shed or chicken coop. Dog hairs and bantie feathers were later found stuck to the oily mouths of the jugs. The brothers stored the filled jugs in a wooden crate lined with an old copy of the *Redding Record Searchlight*.

Except for the most primitive examples (a two-liter plastic soda bottle slipped over a gun muzzle), most Internet designs for homemade silencers follow a perforated tube-within-a-tube pattern. You can use PVC pipe or radiator hose or motorcycle brake tubes. The damping material can be steel wool or cotton or Chore Boy sponges or rags. You can get fancy with a lathe and washers, but Matthew didn't bother. His silencer was fitted to a .22-caliber automatic, not his Glock.

---

3. It seems the Columbine massacre was meant to take place on April 19th, not on the 20th, either to spare a student who was supposed absent that day or to commemorate or rival the burning of the Branch Davidian compound on that day in 1993 and the Oklahoma City bombing, also on the 19th, in 1995. The idea of wearing trench coats may have come from a fantasy scene in *The Basketball Diaries* (1995) in which Leonardo DiCaprio wears a trench coat and shoots classmates. The point is that widespread *speculation* about Columbine could have had eerie resonance for Matthew, who'd begun his "war" on the day of the massacre, who *was* commemorating Hitler's birthday, and who had likely been impressed by *The Matrix*.

Around June 16, the brothers bought a new black crowbar and a black pry bar. They would wear blue mechanic's jumpsuits on their mission. In an interview later, Tyler said Gary Matson and Winfield Mowder came up now as possible targets.

Gary Matson was fifty. He had a mustache, wire-rimmed aviator glasses, a tonsured-looking baldness with a flyaway fringe of blond hair, and the untidy wardrobe of a gardener. He seemed in serious need of gay style advice. He would have shrugged. The son of a college professor and a knowledge geek himself, he was too busy reading botanical journals, teaching, gathering material for a book on local flora. He was a resolutely local and neighborly sort of public figure.

He'd had a hippie phase, hair to his shoulder blades. Back then he fathered a daughter, Clea, with his wife Marcia Howe. The couple started a food coop, People of Progress, and later helped found the Redding Certified Farmer's Market. Gary was the force behind a children's natural history museum in Caldwell Park in Redding where Marcia became director. Through People of Progress Gary started a community garden on the Sacramento River. He got a ten-acre arboretum going on city-owned property. He earned a little money on the side with a specialty nursery.

Winfield Mowder, who was ten years younger, lived with Gary in a ramshackle property on rural Olive Street in an area called Happy Valley, south of Redding. They'd been together fourteen years. Winfield worked at Orchard Hardware Supply in Redding while he studied for a higher degree at Chico State. He was bearded, chunky, an environmentalist nerd like Gary, a cheerful eternal student to Gary's natural teacher.

Gary Matson and Matthew Williams probably met when Matthew joined the Redding Certified Farmer's Market. By all accounts they never knew each other well. Still, they must have had a few conversations. Gary may have taken Matthew to Olive Street, shown off what he was growing there, or loaned Matthew a book. A market acquaintance was later quoted: "I believe Matthew talked about how intelligent Gary was." Whether Matthew ever met Winfield isn't known. He learned the two men were gay, though.

Olin Gordon, an elderly man from Olinda, right next to Happy Valley, considered hiring Matthew and Tyler. The fifteen dollars an hour Matthew asked for sounded steep. Just shooting the breeze, the eighty-six-year-old recalled wondering, "You know Gary Matson—does the same sort of work?"

"Yeah, I know him," Matthew answered. "He's a homosexual."

Gordon tried to explain it to a reporter later. He was old enough to remember when saying something like that amounted to a serious charge. Even now, it felt odd hearing it in normal conversation. Whose business was it?

Redding is so conservative that Gary's daughter never dared tell her religious classmates about her father and Winfield. Maybe there were no other obvious gay people in town. Maybe Gary was the only out gay man Matthew encountered there. Regardless, when Matthew felt he had to make a "judgment" on homosexuality, Gary was the one.

Matthew and Tyler's "war" was to have more than one front: homosexuals, abortionists, Jews. Matthew had assembled a list of nationally prominent Jews on his computer.

The brothers must have practiced. The night of the first attack would involve split-second timing. They'd have to drive from address to address without making a false turn. Just choosing the first night's targets had to involve research.

As the brothers waited for the day they'd chosen, the oddly elegiac alertness of soldiers probably came over them. Matthew would have seen three days of front-page articles in the *Record Searchlight* about the capture of Kathleen Ann Soliah in Minnesota. If nothing else, the story proved that it was possible to live underground for twenty-three years, marry, have a family. Heartening for someone about to become a fugitive.

Friday, June 18 had symbolic weight. On that date in 1984, "The Order" assassinated the radio host Alan Berg in Denver as part of their own legendary racial holy war. A little after midnight Matthew and Tyler left Palo Cedro and took I-5 south to Sacramento, a two-and-a-half-hour trip. The freeway runs through downtown Sacramento, hugging the eastern bank of the Sacramento River. Passing the vivid yellow-orange Tower Bridge, aglow in streetlight at that quiet hour, the brothers headed into south Sacramento and got off the highway at the Sutterville Road exit. They drove north on Riverside Boulevard, which doubles back along I-5 for a while before veering right to pass in front of William Land Park.

They pulled the car into the shadow of one of the great trees near the park entrance. They would have been on the right side of the street. On the left, on a triangle of land cut off in back by the I-5, was Congregation B'nai Israel's synagogue complex—sanctuary, chapel, education wing, courtyard, and library. The famously progressive B'nai Israel was founded in 1852; it's the oldest congregation in Sacramento and one of the oldest in the American West.

Matthew used the crate in which they'd stored the oil jugs. He packed several of the jugs inside, tossed the crowbar on top, and scuttled across the street. Park, synagogue, and neighborhood were utterly deserted. It was a quarter past three in the morning.

Matthew set the crate down by a metal door just off the street, a door he'd likely examined already. He used the crowbar to pop it open. The alarm sounded at three nineteen a.m. He described it to a reporter later. Though he was denying Tyler's involvement at the time—claiming instead that he worked with those eight unnamed guys— his description of the moment was probably true: "I was real nervous. Getting caught was a real issue. Just the excitement of it, coming in and having the alarm go off, and I knew I was crossing the Rubicon. It was the cusp of my life where I was putting faith in my beliefs." The immediate reality may have been darker, terrifying and exhilarating. He was on Satan's ground.

He grabbed the jugs and hustled through the library. He smashed a window to get out of the locked vestibule and found the sanctuary. You can imagine him in there. When he unscrewed one jug, the cap jumped from his fingers. It was found later. With a sowing motion of the arm he poured the sputtering liquid from the jug. He splashed a piano, the benches, the walls. He ran to the front of the sanctuary and splashed the bimah. He ignited the fires with an electronic stick lighter. After an irritating crackling like loose wax in the ear came the wonderful thud and windy heat. He tossed the plastic jug aside, though he'd meant to take it with him.

On his way back out he doused the library. This time he did a more thorough job. The sanctuary fire was already beginning to burn out. Here he soaked the books and got a real fire going. This building would be gutted. Again, he dropped the jug. He ran out, leaping past the crate, though he'd meant to take that with him too. From the moment he left the car to the moment he jumped back in, only three or four minutes had passed. The burglar alarm registered automatically at three twenty-four a.m. The brothers were gone.

Congregation Beth Shalom, another Reform synagogue, is on El Camino Avenue in Carmichael, at the other end of Sacramento, an off-white stucco A-frame facing the street. A big flame-shaped sign carries the congregation's name (*House of Peace*) in Hebrew. The best way to get there from B'nai Israel is to go north past the Riverside Water Treatment Plant and take the eastbound Capitol City/El Dorado Freeway. Exiting the freeway you have to cross the river and take one of the big streets north to El Camino. Or the brothers could have turned around and gotten back on the northbound I-5, then traveled one of the major arteries east as if they were heading to Cal Expo. Either route takes just over twenty minutes. There was no traffic, but they would have avoided speeding. The timing just works out. The Beth Shalom alarm registered at three forty-eight a.m.

The shul of the Kenesset Israel Torah Center is four miles from Beth Shalom on quiet Morse Avenue. The alarm at this Orthodox synagogue went off a bare ten minutes after the Beth Shalom alarm. That means Matthew must have broken in, set his fire (Beth Shalom suffered mostly sprinkler damage), and traveled the four miles on El Camino and Watt Avenue within that time. It's possible. The shul suffered mostly smoke damage. Still, the building had to be replaced. Here, Matthew remembered to take in some of his anti-Semitic fliers and scatter them around. His palm print was later found on one. The brothers were back in Palo Cedro by six thirty a.m. Friday morning, unless they stopped at Matthew's Redding apartment to recover.

This time people noticed. The synagogue arsons were national news. The city was appalled. Because the fires seemed nearly simultaneous, the early impression was that a squad of arsonists had fanned out through the city. Rewards were offered, a unity rally was held in the Sacramento Community Center, the FBI gathered evidence, and B'nai Israel started accepting replacement volumes for its ruined library and holding summer services in a recently opened courtyard.

People studied the fliers left behind. "The ugly American and NATO aggressors are the ultimate hypocrites. The fake Albanian refugee crisis was manufactured by the international Jewsmedia to justify the terrorizing, the bestial bombing of our Yugoslavia back into the dark ages." The author was referring to the bombing campaign against Serbia. The campaign had been prompted by the flight from Kosovo of almost half a million people in fear of ethnic cleansing. The author's passions had been excited by a terrifying but remote and hard-to-fathom event. Like any underground extremist, his truth was simplified and inverted. What connection could he have found between the synagogues of Sacramento and the mosques of Tirana? This combination of intensity and obscurity is typical of Matthew.

The usual suspects were questioned by reporters. William Pierce in West Virginia knew nothing about it. Matthew Hale, then running the World Church of the Creator out of his father's basement in East Peoria, Illinois, said his organization didn't promote violence, though it was hard to object to someone torching the "dens of the serpent."

Matthew and Tyler laid low through the weekend and the next week. For the first time Matthew could view his actions projected on the screen of genuine notoriety (not just an article about Living Faith in the *Moscow-Pullman Daily News*, not just a self-published health guide). This was national. Q-scored faces spoke with expressions of compassionate woe, local TV reporters interviewed congregants. The inevitable inaccuracy and the artificial emotionalism of American news must only have reinforced Matthew's delusion that the world was a *Matrix*-like lie. He couldn't be touched. What he didn't believe in wasn't real. Far from having the slightest twinge of remorse, he started compiling an additional list of prominent local Jews. The list was afterward found on his computer by the FBI. Following the name of a man who'd offered a reward for the arsonists' capture, he noted, "Yidbizman, $10,000 on us." He later said the first attack emboldened him.

The brothers waited through a second weekend. All this time, eleven days, they only had themselves to talk to about what had happened. Did they debrief in a military fashion? Discuss upcoming plans? Did Ben or Sally ever mention the Sacramento attacks? Did the parents notice their sons seemed . . . silent? Energized?

On the last day of June, a Wednesday, Winfield Mowder and Gary Matson had dinner with Gary's father, Oscar, a widower for seven years now. Oscar once taught German, French, Spanish, and English at Shasta College but he was best-known as a vintner. The family business, Matson Vineyards, founded in 1984, was the oldest in Shasta County. It was east of Redding, a stone's throw from the Williams place in Palo Cedro.

Gary and Winfield left at about eleven and headed home to Olive Street in Happy Valley. Sometime during the first hours of July 1, Matthew and Tyler drove their father's Toyota Corolla hatchback over to Olive Street, probably taking the exact same route Gary and Winfield had driven earlier.

The couple's house, an unselfconsciously rundown trailer with a big one-room living space added on, was about halfway along Olive Street. Coming from the south, there were indeed neatly spaced olive trees growing on either side of the road. Farther along, the withered-looking trunks of eucalyptus raised their feathery crowns much higher against the starry sky. A waning gibbous moon had been full two nights before. The earthen roadsides were dry and yellow. The air smelled of eucalyptus and the vaguely horsey dust of a long, intensely hot day.

Matthew and Tyler probably pulled off onto a dirt road or alongside an olive grove; they wouldn't have driven right up to the house. They let their eyes adjust to the darkness. Olive Street is rural, unlit, with a number of widely separated houses (none as ramshackle as Gary and Winfield's).

As it was described to me, you entered the house and found yourself in the main living space. Kitchen and bathroom were in the trailer section. Matthew may have known the layout already. Directly opposite the door was a big, roughly built loft bed running sideways along the far wall. There were flimsy bookshelves with more books and botanical journals scattered across the floor. The place was a mess, either waiting for a big cleanup or, more likely, treated with indifference by the intellectual couple.

They were asleep in the loft bed, naked, Winfield on the near side, Gary by the wall. Maybe they stirred at the sound of the door opening. Maybe not. Tyler has said he didn't remember either of them sitting up or saying anything. Whatever the plan had been, Matthew acted precipitately. He got a foot or two inside the door. This was it. He raised the .22 and started firing. The silencer made a prim farting sound, but the brass shell casings pinged and danced on the floor. Matthew pumped about fifteen shots into the two men. All Tyler remembered was a soft groan or sigh when the bodies deflated slightly and relaxed into death.

Matthew may have used an entire clip, normally ten to fifteen shells. If so, he had to put another clip in. He moved a chair to the foot of the loft bed. He stood on the seat, steadied himself, and fired several more times into the motionless bodies—kill shots. Just to be sure. Atomized blood spit back from the close-range wounds and flecked the silencer. Matthew jumped down. (There has been speculation that Tyler fired some or all of the shots, because his prints were found on the gun later. I've tried to contact him several times with no success. My hunch is that Matthew would have taken the lead throughout.)

The brothers went through the pockets of the pants Gary had slung aside before going to bed. They took his car keys and a Visa card. As part of the plan—unless they were improvising on the fly—they were going to take Gary's bronze Toyota Tercel wagon. But what if someone noticed it was missing? They did something that probably felt clever—even brilliant—given the panicky state they were in.

Gary and Winfield had an old answering machine, the

kind with a miniature cassette tape for the outgoing message. The brothers erased the message and recorded a new one. Matthew coughs a few times to mimic illness then mumbles, "Uh, hi, this is Gary . . ." *Cough, cough.* "Gary" says he isn't feeling well. "We're going to, uh, visit a specialist friend in San Francisco for a week."

The brothers were too wired to replay the message to make it sure it sounded right. Otherwise, they would have noticed that lagging spools or sticky buttons had caused a problem. When the tape is played, you first hear, "*Be-e-e-e-e-e-ep!*" Then Tyler's voice, "—make it any longer than you have to." And only then, *Cough, cough.* "Uh, hi, this is Gary . . ."

A couple of things about this message . . . First, it's ludicrous. The childish pretense of illness and the equally childish "specialist friend" and gay men/San Francisco association make for a ridiculous ploy. Only someone with a contemptuous or unrealistic streak a mile wide could think it passable. Did Matthew believe his victims were rarely telephoned, marginal, friendless? Did he think callers would shrug when they heard a message like that? Did he think the unprepossessing shanty they lived in meant Gary and Winfield would be considered socially disposable?

Far stranger (even if recording that message was part of the plan from the beginning), Matthew chose to impersonate Gary moments after killing him, a man with whom he shared more than a few points in common. (Both were gifted horticulturists. Both had a BA in biology and the instincts of a teacher. Both were overqualified for the labor they loved as nurserymen/gardeners. Both had one daughter.) No matter how rushed, how nervous, how frazzled, how drunk on glory, how numbed by exhilaration, some kind of existential weirdness must have flickered through Matthew for an instant when he said, "This is Gary."

That's not him, Oscar Matson thought as soon as he heard the message. He'd phoned the next morning. Worried, he asked his son Roger, an enologist at the vineyard, to check on Gary and Winfield. By one o'clock, Roger was at the Olive Street house, probably calling out and hearing the nervousness in his own voice. He noticed the car was missing. He pushed open the door, saw several shell casings and, looking up, the bodies in the loft bed.

Tyler had taken their father's car back to Palo Cedro. Matthew had driven Gary's either to Palo Cedro or to his Hartnell Avenue apartment in Redding. Over the next day the car must have been a source of worry. The fact that they had it, and might as well use it, may have hastened the next attack.

If Matthew was able to sleep at all that morning, he was up by three p.m. at the latest. He had no reason to believe the bodies had been discovered two hours earlier. But he seems to have been in a hurry now, expanding his plans. At three he called Dillon Precision Products Inc. in Scottsdale, Arizona. Dillon is the country's premier maker of reloading equipment. The Dillon 550 and the Dillon 650 may be the best machines available for making cartridges, a thriving hobby among people who are cost-conscious, finicky, or private when it comes to their ammo. Besides the press, you need a proper set of dyes for the caliber cartridges you want to make. You can take used shell casings, recharge the case with gunpowder, and seat and crimp a new bullet. Matthew ordered one of the machines along with some expensive accessories. He also ordered two classic black-leather gun belts, waist size 32" for himself, 34" for Tyler.

The total came to $2,276.09. He used Gary Matson's Visa card and gave a Mailboxes Etc. box number as the delivery address. The initial weirdness of impersonating Gary may have passed by now.

Sometime after midnight, Matthew and Tyler headed back downstate to Sacramento. They started out in two cars, parked one somewhere, and continued on in Gary's Tercel wagon. They'd already chosen a target, but they wanted to act at once and get rid of the car. Or else, after killing two people the night before, continued warfare felt paradoxically more bearable than time to reflect.

They got to Sacramento at their usual action hour, three a.m. They drove to a shopping center called Country Club Plaza on the corner of El Camino and Watt Avenue. This is exactly halfway between Beth Shalom and the Kenesset Israel Torah Center. They'd passed the shopping center at around three fifty-six a.m. twelve nights before. Now they were back, a military-style runaround tactic. Behind the shopping center on Butano Drive is the Country Club Medical Center, on the second floor of which was the Choice Medical Group, an abortion clinic, tonight's target.

This time Matthew used the pry bar. He had trouble getting the green aluminum door to pop open, so he smashed an upper pane of glass. The laminated glass shattered but hung from the frame. Matthew threw one of his lighted incendiaries inside. He smashed windows at two of the building's three other entrances and chucked in more Molotov cocktails. He had one left. Running behind the building he threw it into a green garbage bin.

It was three twenty. A sanitation worker pulled a truck around the back of the building and saw the bin in flames. Startled by motion, he spotted two men in jumpsuits getting into a boxy car. Under the deceiving parking lot lights the car's copper paint job was an indefinite muddy color. And anyway, it was gone before the garbage collector registered what was going on. The fire department came. The fire was out within twenty minutes. The Choice Medical Group offices hadn't been touched.

Nothing was reported on the Redding murders for several days. Investigators thought it was a local case, ugly but not earth-shaking. No connection was made to Sacramento, of course. And no connection was made between the clinic firebombing and the synagogues. Not that every article didn't mention both or ask the question, "Any connection?" At one point, investigators suspected the owner of the clinic building was responsible himself—insurance fraud. Also, three different jurisdictions were involved: ATF at the clinic arson, FBI at the synagogues, and the Shasta County Sheriff's Department on Olive Street.

Something feels incomplete, exhausted, about the clinic attack. Even so, Matthew and Tyler were probably confident of their safety. With no reason to believe the Olive Street scene had been discovered, they may have thought their answering machine ploy had worked. They tried to rest. But they weren't finished. This was still just the beginning.

The evening of that same day, July 2, in Chicago, "August" Benjamin Nathaniel Smith, until recently a member of the World Church of the Creator and a close associate of church leader Matt Hale, started shooting Orthodox Jewish men walking home from Sabbath services. It was the start of a three-day spree. After wounding six in Chicago, Smith drove to Skokie and murdered ex-basketball coach Ricky Byrdsong. If Matthew or Tyler napped that afternoon, they may have woken up to breaking news about these racist attacks and thought, *If this isn't the beginning of a racial holy war . . .*

Smith threaded a path between Illinois and Indiana over the next two days, killed a Korean student, shot or shot at six others, then shot himself while being chased on I-57 near Salem, Illinois. He was captured in a messy struggle during which he shot himself again. He died in a hospital. It was the Fourth of July.

One small item didn't make the news: California police discovered Gary Matson's Tercel wagon at two p.m. on July 3. The car was abandoned in Oroville, California, a little up-country from Gridley. When officers opened the car, they noticed a strong odor of gasoline.

Many murder cases are easy to solve. Forensics is about proof not clues. The killing of Gary and Winfield, however, was genuinely mysterious. Even after the car was found in Oroville, investigators had a difficult time imagining a story line. The victims were paradigmatic innocents, beloved and without an enemy in the world. Just when the police were at a loss how to proceed, they were alerted that Gary's credit card had been used. The reloading equipment had shipped. Dillon gave the authorities the delivery address.

Yuba City (where Sally Williams once taught elementary school) isn't far from Oroville. So that seemed to fit. The Mailboxes Etc. store was in the Feather Down Shopping Center, a sprawling pink strip mall, its façade hinting at '80s postmodernism. On a hot Wednesday afternoon, July 7, cops showed up to ask about "Gary Matson's" box. The man at the counter looked up from his computer screen. With a shrug of surprise, he gestured through the plate glass: well, there they are! Two young men had just gotten out of a Corolla hatchback and were approaching the store.

Shouting, guns drawn, officers pushed open the door. Matthew and Tyler took a few steps back toward the car. Other policemen materialized. With a glance of assessment, they too drew their guns and aimed at the young men. All were close enough to hear Matthew quietly ask Tyler, "Well, partner, what are we gonna do?"

The capture was a matter of dumb luck for the police and startlingly abrupt. If any of the officers had doubts, they disappeared as soon as the suspects were searched. The police found that Matthew was wearing a bulletproof vest. He had his Glock on him. Tyler was carrying a 9mm handgun, as well. Inside the car were two assault rifles, two more handguns, a shotgun, a pry bar, a crowbar, a homemade silencer speckled with something, blood it turned out. On the floor by the driver's seat, an extra set of car keys was found—Gary's. And they found Gary's Visa card. The card was the pretext for arrest: possession of stolen property.

The capture took place at four thirty in the afternoon. Then a grueling full day's worth of legal procedures began. Matthew and Tyler weren't booked in the Shasta County Jail until one fifteen a.m. Bail was set at two million each. Obviously, the authorities had more on their minds than possession of stolen property.

III. Escape

The Shasta County Jail was built in 1984. A boxy eleven-story building of stained concrete, it's fittingly ugly for a prison, a heavy-browed, slit-eyed modernist mug of a structure. Inside, mottled concrete floors as dark as pumice have been rubbed smooth by jail-issue slippers and flip-flops. The cinder-block walls are painted the color of dirty pollen. The paint's been scratched away from pipes and vent covers by anxious prisoners. Scablike patches of metal show through. Prison clothing comes in two colors, pale tangerine for T-shirts, socks, briefs, and slippers; black for the pajama-like pants and a V-necked pullover. In the visitor's room and dayroom the seats are immovable discs of stainless steel projecting from under stainless steel tables. Visitors are allowed the usual telephone conversation through a glass window.

On Thursday evening, July 8, Sally Williams finally got to speak to Matthew.

"I still love you," she told her son at once.

"I love you too."

Sally sighed. "I don't know. It looks real bad."

Matthew diverted her. Or maybe he couldn't help himself. What's a mother for, if not complaint? He said they took some cash and tools from him. They had him on suicide watch. They also took away his socks. He was freezing. (The building had been refitted in '97 to operate two chillers on hot days, part of an energy-efficient HVAC system.)

Matthew tried to reassure her. "Our forefathers have been in prison a lot—prophets, Christ."

Sally told him she'd start looking for a lawyer.

"Don't bother," Matthew shot back. "I plan to represent myself from Scriptures."

"I don't think you did what they say you did," Sally said earnestly.

"What do they say I did?"

"They say you took out two homos." Sally said she

couldn't imagine him doing something like that.

Matthew responded callously, "Why wouldn't you think I'd do that?" He continued, "I had to obey God's law rather than man's law. I didn't want to do this. I felt I was supposed to, though . . . They're not doing the death penalty a whole lot here anymore. I'm probably looking at twenty, forty years. I don't think I'll serve that, though."

He seems to be equating assassination with a bar fight gone wrong, but he likely couldn't grasp what even those numbers sounded like to a mother. Or what they could mean for a man.

Matthew said, "I think God put me here as a witness. A lot of people will hear. They call what I've done bad . . . I've followed a higher law . . . People will hear it. They might think I'm insane . . . I see a lot of parallels between this and a lot of other incidents in the Old Testament. They threw our Lord Savior in jail."

Only after Matthew and Tyler were captured did the investigation finally come together. What was a Redding newspaper, the one lining the crate left at B'nai Israel, doing in Sacramento? Why the odor of gasoline in Gary's car? When Matthew's Hartnell Avenue apartment was searched (after the street was blocked off for fear of explosives), investigators came across reams of hate literature, more weapons, the list of prominent Jews.

At Palo Cedro, a crate like the B'nai Israel one was discovered, plus Mobil Delvac 1300 jugs identical to those left behind by the arsonist. Dog hairs and chicken feathers were collected. A blue jumpsuit of Tyler's was found, and fibers linked it to the upholstery of Gary's car. Paint and glass powder on the pry bar and crowbar were examined.

As the forensic evidence fell into place, dread rippled outward. Just how big was this thing? Matthew and Tyler had successfully conjured at least the impression of a war.

There'd been another murder in Happy Valley a month earlier. A mistaken report got out that the victim had been shot, so the killing sounded like the Olive Street murders. And if Matthew and Tyler weren't involved in that one, what about the young man who'd gone missing in the Pullman-Moscow area back when Matthew was living in the Palouse?

More alarming than the stray unsolved case was the illusion of conspiracy. A lot remained unclear about Columbine. The Southern Poverty Law Center and other activist groups had been warning that extremists might engage in year-2000 domestic terrorism. Benjamin Smith's Midwestern racist spree had coincided precisely with the Williams brothers' attacks. Matthew's letter to William Pierce and World Church of the Creator literature were found along with everything else at Hartnell Avenue. Could this be part of a nationwide plot cooked up by the odious Matt Hale or someone like him?

Hate groups, by their nature, can thrive without conspiracies, without organization of any kind. The same sacred texts are available to everyone: *The Protocols of the Elders of Zion*, *The Turner Diaries*, Resistance Records' music, old issues of *Racial Loyalty*, Nord Davis's *Star Wars*, handbooks on incendiaries and silencers and explosives, *Israel: Our Duty, Our Dilemma*. Like the kit houses the Sears catalog once flogged all over America, kit ideology can be mailed or downloaded anywhere. Some of the things Matthew did— leafleting high schools, sharing important books, dropping the leading inquiry ("What do you think of black people?"

he once asked Jeff Monroe)—come straight from the racist playbook for recruitment, instructions he might have read somewhere and followed with soldierly fervor. A much-discussed theory even describes how concerted action is generated without organization: the "propaganda of the deed" is supposed to galvanize sympathizers into acting on their own. Matthew was probably convinced it would work for him.

Matthew shaved his head before his first court appearance, a preliminary hearing on July 13. The hearing lasted five and three-quarters hours. Ben and Sally attended, sitting impassively. Prosecutors played a scratchy recording of the July 8 prison conversation (quoted above from newspaper accounts). Sally and Matthew had overlooked a posted warning that conversations could be recorded. Spectators gasped at Sally's "They say you took out two homos." Fleeting as it was, there was the proof of hatred. Afterward, someone shouted at Sally that Gary and Winfield had been better men than her monstrous sons . . . The calm of proceedings like these sometimes feels outrageous. The formal repression of the courtroom must have made grief almost unendurable for the friends and family of Winfield and Gary.

Strangely enough, this was only the start of the most important part of Matthew's life. It wasn't denouement. Though he was thirty-one, like many adolescents he'd lived a fantasy life so far. Now, just when his fantasies seemed to have come true, he was also facing the disillusionment of real life. Real life ends up out-arguing all of us. You can't catch its eye and charm it. And this wasn't the usual real life of jobs and disappointment, it was imprisonment, the relentless, hard-hearted, small-minded necessity of the law.

Matthew's emotions apparently whipsawed between intoxication with his fame and the petty humiliations of life in the Shasta County Jail. Unlike in movies, real life doesn't cue your doom with music. Early on, the familiar-from-TV routine of prison, the apparently humdrum personalities of the inmates and prison staff, the sheer banality of it all, may have led Matthew to believe this was going to be a breeze. He thought he was the smartest guy around, and maybe he was. He was prey to a cocky adolescent hilarity. One of the first things he sent from jail in July or August was a credit card application on which he described his "employment." He wrote, "My brother and I were captured by occupation storm troopers while we were on a supply mission. We are now incarcerated for our work in cleansing a sick society."

Matthew became the demonic darling of reporters. No matter how silly, contemptible, or emotionally disconnected, everything he said was treated with gravity. Since it's unbearable for most of us to think that evil has silly, contemptible, and emotionally disconnected causes (though it almost always does), reporters, in spite of themselves, inflated Matthew's importance. His immaturity was painted as satanic levity. Although in his own mind he was playing *Braveheart* and made an effort to get that image out there, he must have known he was swimming against a tide of disapproval. He wrote frequent letters to the *Redding Record Searchlight* and the *Sacramento Bee*. One included a plaintive-sounding, "I'm not a hate-filled man."

At the same time, Matthew had always been eager to please. His instinct was to reward anyone smitten with him. It's hard not to think he unconsciously played to the "monster" expectations of the reporters who were suddenly so interested in him. Jeff Monroe recalls seeing courtroom footage of Matthew smirking into the camera, eyes going narrow like a comic book villain's. *I don't know this man,* Jeff tells me he thought in shock. It didn't occur to him that "Evil Matthew" and the old "Endearing Matthew" of the Palouse were equally unreal, the operatic sham behavior of someone who hasn't grown up, who doesn't know himself at all.

Matthew was prepared to say anything to entertain his audience and did. He confessed. His lawyer was exasperated. Despite a passing whim (a joke?) to appear in court in a Nazi uniform and wearing a toothbrush mustache, Matthew was determined to stick to his plan of representing himself from Scripture. It felt like a bold and idealistic stand, and it demanded confession. But confessing was probably also a way of reassuring himself that his own foolishness—his crime—had been a coherent intention all along. Because if he started gleaning that it wasn't . . . Bizarrely, confessing likely *postponed* any horrible "real life" understanding of what he'd done.

Gary Delsohn and Sam Stanton were reporters for the *Sacramento Bee*. On November 4 they came to the jail to interview Matthew and found him smug and relaxed. Delsohn held the phone in the visiting room. They were talking in circles. Fed up with the verbal sparring, Stanton tells me he grabbed the phone and demanded, "Did you do it?"

Matthew wasn't going to pause or appear the least bit unsure of himself. He answered at once, "Absolutely." He told the two reporters, "I'm not guilty of murder. I'm guilty of obeying the laws of the Creator."

Stanton and Delsohn had gotten the headline they wanted and continued to follow the case doggedly. They weren't the only ones fascinated by the case. *Dateline NBC* and *60 Minutes* did segments on the Williams brothers. Matthew was interviewed a great deal. Famously, he and Tom Brokaw had a heated exchange during an interview. There was no breaking through Matthew's glibness. It must have given the young man a sense of triumph to get under the skin of the star newsman from Babylon on the Hudson. Brokaw was faced with the brick wall pseudosophistication of an overgrown, self-convinced adolescent.

Matthew was famous. He was contacted by the cultural lurkers drawn to grisly notoriety. In December he sent a drawing to a collector of memorabilia of famous killers. In some ways he was having fun. He decorated the envelope with a glowing key and the racist catchphrase "fourteen words" transliterated into runes. ("Fourteen words" refers to a credo dreamed up by The Order's David Lane: "We must secure the existence of our people and a future for white children.") Matthew delighted in getting secret messages past the jail censors. He became furious when he learned that Ann and Jeff Monroe had spoken to the FBI and viciously sent them an article on obesity, adding a series of biblical citations that amounted to a death threat. It was the last they ever heard from him.

He was famous, but he was also powerless. He was kept in "administrative segregation." Ad-seg is highly controlled imprisonment away from the general inmate population. A fellow inmate told me deputies gave Matthew a hard time. Perhaps they spread rumors about him and tried to create conflict. Perhaps they laughed at his beliefs or passed along the by-now-widespread speculation that Matthew was gay himself. The fellow inmate told me deputies continually wrote Matthew up for petty violations of jail rules—having too many pairs of socks, too many letters, being disrespectful. He says Matthew was kept in more or less permanent lockdown with these violations.

Matthew's name changed in prison. After the crimes he became known in police papers and court filings by the name on his birth certificate, Benjamin Matthew Williams. Tyler was James Tyler Williams. Newspaper articles had to explain repetitively that the brothers went by their middle names. But in prison Matthew accepted that he was Ben now, exactly like his father. Deputies and inmates called him Ben, and he started signing drawings and letters "Benjamin XIV Williams" or "Benjamin Matthew XIV Williams," sometimes specifying, "Rev XIV.12." ("Here is the patience of the saints, those who keep the commandments of God, and the faith of Jesus." Revelations XIV is a vision of the angels of the Apocalypse with whom Ben apparently identified himself.)

But prison began to wear him down. In November the Shasta County DA McGregor Scott decided to go for the death penalty for both brothers. When Stanton and Delsohn interviewed him again on January 6, Ben appeared nervous. His hand shook when he held the telephone, and when they asked about the death penalty decision, he admitted, "Tyler has been pretty upset about it."

The arsons were first to come to trial in federal court. The murders wouldn't be dealt with in state court for a year or two. The frenzy of media curiosity abated. Prison, even if it hadn't seemed so awesome initially, must have started to look far more imposing with the dimension of time factored in.

The tedious courtroom routine quashed Ben's theatrical attempt to defend himself from Scripture. His lawyer had the impossible job of representing someone who'd quite sanely admitted the crimes he was accused of. In fact, the Bible *was* the only defense in this case. Ben was right about that.

An effort to bring religion into the trial may have been behind a bizarre episode a few days after Father's Day. On Sunday, June 18, 2000, Oscar Matson, seventy-seven now, turned a page of the *Redding Record Searchlight* and found the following ad illustrated with a dove holding an olive branch:

> *Congratulations! The family and friends of Benjamin Matthew Williams are proud to announce that he was ordained Reverend by Christ's Covenant Church. This honor was bestowed as recognition of his decade of diligent studies in Ancient Wisdom and Truth and for his spiritual works benefiting our fellowship and community. Reverend Williams: May your knowledge and faith continue to grow during your current persecutions and trials.*

The newspaper hastily apologized for running the small ad. Reporters tracked down the purchaser—Ben's lawyer. If he meant to set up an argument that religious freedom or religious mania were somehow behind the crimes, it was wasted effort. The courts wouldn't allow a defense based on the holy book of a five-thousand-year-old desert tribe.

Ben made at least one friend in jail. Twenty-four-year-old Paul Gordon Smith Jr., known as PJ, was in ad-seg too. A ward of the court since he was five, PJ had spent most of his life in institutions of one kind or another. Now he was charged with the gruesome murder of a young woman. In ad-seg, prisoners are usually allowed out of their cells for an hour a day unless they're in lockdown. Ben and PJ got to talking in the common area and hit it off at once, according to PJ.

PJ says he never bought into Ben's constant talk about religion, nor did he get Ben's visceral revulsion for homosexuality. They became friends because they were starved for intelligent company. They talked science. Or Ben would describe episodes of his Edenic childhood, and PJ couldn't help envying what sounded to him like an ideal family life. Time began to loom large. A year passed. The federal trial was drawing to a close.

Even though some of Ben's letters and drawings reflect strict Christian Identity beliefs, PJ is adamant that Ben's beliefs were free-form and more diverse and, most interesting, that they were changing. Ben talked and wrote about American Indian spirituality, Druidic religion, even Wicca. Similar references had appeared in the old pamphlet "Optimum Health and Longevity." Ben's hatred of homosexuality itself may have been wearing thin. One wonders whether his beliefs weren't supremely incoherent all along. He may always have been too impatient to let his beliefs gel before inspiration became action. Or maybe his beliefs were fundamentally exterior to him: a book, a mentor, a father, a mother. Those of us hoping to figure it all out may be trying to attribute logic to notions of honor, self, and world as wild as love. But PJ claims that prison was changing Ben to the core. He says at the end Ben didn't even consider himself Christian.

And while he acknowledges the irony that the worst homophobes do sometimes turn out to be gay, PJ says simply, "Ben wasn't gay." The idea that he was came up because it always comes up. It strikes some people as perversely fitting.

That old hiking friend from the Palouse, Dan Martin, also gave the idea a boost. In the early months after the crimes and before dropping out of sight, Martin gave an interview to the gay magazine the *Advocate*. The article reports that Matthew (as he was known in Idaho) went skinny-dipping and wrote poetry with his best friend, who later turned out to be gay. "You do the math," the article suggested.

Both the *Bee* reporter Sam Stanton and Jeff Monroe to this day wonder whether Matthew was confused about his sexuality. Both mentioned it to me. But Stanton and Monroe are straight. For them, there's a vengeful neatness to the story if Matthew/Ben was gay. And Dan Martin, who is gay, probably always saw his friend through a lens of fondness. Also, he was remembering a time when his own sexuality wasn't clear to him. Nothing but hope or innuendo says Ben was gay. He wasn't. However upsetting the realization—and we're right to be upset, because this is an authentic instance of hatred that can't be psychologized away—an idea of what's right, not simple emotion, caused him to kill.

According to PJ the subject was in the air from the start. Both were up for the death penalty, and soon they started talking about escape.

The jail was beginning to show its age. In addition to revamping the air-conditioning system, authorities were making other improvements. A catwalk had been added to the second tier of the ad-seg "pod," 3C. A secure door was placed right in front of the upstairs shower. From there, the catwalk led to the "mod," the control area for corrections officers. With the new catwalk built, officers had direct access to both levels of the pod and wouldn't have to climb the stairs inside the housing unit to reach the upper tier.

In any ad hoc design, compromises are made. It was hard for observant prisoners not to notice that the new catwalk leading to the mod also led right to an exterior window over the jail's garage. If you could get through the secure door, somehow get past security cameras, somehow break the window, somehow get safely down to the garage roof, then to the street . . . That was the plan.

PJ tells me Ben was impatient. He seemed to think all they needed to do was get into the mod. Then everything would work out. PJ was more cautious. They had to study the mod schedules and weather reports. There's a hint of wistfulness in PJ's description of their planned route. They meant to use side roads to drive up to the Oregon/Nevada/ California border. They'd go in summer, because winter wouldn't allow for easy movement. Still, they'd have to watch for good weather throughout Idaho and up into Canada. They decided the smart, counterintuitive destination would be someplace remote, not a densely populated area. Behind the plan one can almost hear Ben's romantic descriptions of the wilds around Ruby Ridge, his dreams of freedom and solitude in nature. PJ says he kept having to rein in Ben's impulsiveness.

The plan involved a classic element of prison breaks— the rope of sheets knotted together. Late one evening Ben was allowed out of his cell for a shower. He stuffed his clothes on top of the sheet rope in a paper bag and got into the shower wearing only briefs. He didn't shower. He waited past the time he was due back in his cell. Another inmate, Harold Seems, was up for the next shower. PJ assures me Seems took a shower with Ben standing right there the whole time. But Seems later testified that he was in his cell when he heard the following whispered exchange as Ben and PJ walked past:

PJ: *Have you got it?*
Ben: *Yeah.*
PJ: *We're going to have to kill him.*
Ben: *As quick as we can.*

(Seems had to overhear that neatly self-incriminating conversation through a heavy cell door and before the supposed murder weapon was even made, though "it" could refer to a drain cover. The court didn't put too much stress on this part of his testimony.)

At that hour, the jail's main-floor control room was manned, but only individual "prowlers" walked though the pods from time to time, making sure prisoners were where they were supposed to be, handing out medications, or escorting inmates from place to place. According to the deputy in the control room, PJ was let out of his cell between eleven fifty p.m. and one fifteen a.m. At that point he was given extra time to take a shower. So after about quarter past one, Ben and PJ were hiding in the shower together.

There, in wild silence, using his outdoorsman's skills, Ben fashioned a unique tool or weapon to break the window or assault a deputy. A six-inch perforated drain cover had been unscrewed from the floor of his cell but left in place until tonight. A haft was constructed out of rolled paper stiffened with old bars of soap and ballpoint pen refills. Ben folded this around the drain cover, making sure the ends were long enough to provide for a good handle. Using lengths of torn sheet, he sewed the haft to the grill of the drain cover and wrapped the handle tightly. He had to be careful to make the haft secure. Only the curved edge of the drain cover showed past his elaborate weave of knots and ragged stitches. PJ describes him in the shower sewing in feverish haste. The result was a kind of tomahawk. I've seen a photograph of it, bloodied.

The prowler that night was a new guy, the unlucky Timothy Renault, who, incredibly, had had another inmate escape on him two weeks before. Renault was tall, slender, jug-eared. He was only twenty-three and probably still fretting about the coming investigation into the escape. Ben and PJ pressed themselves against the steel walls of the shower. The shower curtain was transparent but so thick and scratched and filmy it was opaque in the shadow. They couldn't see Renault, but they could hear the catwalk door buzz open a mere three feet away. They recognized him by his voice when he keyed the mic at his shoulder to tell control that he'd left the mod. They let him pass. He wasn't the usual guy—too slender, and the plan was to have PJ put on the uniform in case cameras could see them after they bluffed their way into the mod. (As it turned out, the light was so low that cameras wouldn't have made anything out.)

As Renault walked past the cells, he glanced through the tall, narrow windows in each purple-painted door. A letter-sized envelope was wedged in the window frame of Williams's cell, and it looked like the light inside was draped. Renault peered in. It appeared somebody was in the bed. Two envelopes blocked the window of PJ's cell, but someone appeared to be under the blanket in that bed too. The envelopes were a common trick to block light from outside so inmates could sleep.

Ben and PJ let Renault pass a second time. By the third round, it was clear there was no one else to choose. They could hear a tapping from nearby. That would be the cell right next to the shower. It belonged to Harold Seems. Renault's footsteps stopped. He went back past the shower and approached Seems's cell in answer to the tapping. They heard the young deputy ask a question.

Seems later testified that he was at his cell's window, frantic. He gestured toward the mod door. "Get out of here! Get out of here!"

When the situation registered, Renault spun around and made for the mod door. The shower curtain flew open. PJ ran to block the door. He saw Renault key the mic at his shoulder just as the first blow came from behind. PJ and Ben wrestled the deputy down.

Already PJ realized it was too late. He figured Ben hadn't heard the crackle of the mic. He watched his friend chopping in a fury. The radio popped to life asking for a repeat. Still, Ben went on chopping, as if completely possessed by the need to make this work. He and Renault wrestled. The drain-cover blade thudded on bone and clanged against the concrete floor. Lubricated by blood, Renault's hands and boots skated along the floor. According to PJ, Ben's briefs and body were covered with blood. He was a cannibal nightmare, pre-Colombian, pre-Christian, pre-everything.

PJ could hear the elevator now. He knew escape was a lost cause and hurried away from the scene along the upper tier. When the first deputies burst in and spotted him, he raised his hands. A deputy testified that he immediately said, "I didn't do anything. I didn't have anything to do with this. I didn't do anything."

Ben had nearly killed Renault. The young man's skull was fractured in several places, his eye socket and jaw and a tooth were broken. Intracranial bleeding could have injured his brain or caused death. Nine pieces of titanium had to be fitted into his skull to repair the damage. PJ tells me Ben probably thought the deputy would go down with a single blow like on TV. The expectation fits with Ben's dreamy way of seeing the world. Maybe they both thought it would work, but their experiences with murder had been different. PJ knew murder could be hard. When he'd killed, it had been a grueling and horrific act. Ben's murders had been unwontedly easy. He may well have believed—envisioned how—this would be as simple as a scene in *Braveheart*. When reality disappointed him this time, he never recovered.

After the failed escape, PJ was sent to High Desert State Prison. Ben remained in ad-seg and became despondent. It's unlikely that he regretted the attack on Renault. He was as blind as ever to the lives of people around him. But failure itself may have eaten away at him. He wrote in a letter that he felt God had abandoned him because the escape hadn't succeeded.

Ben's amoral religiosity, as well as his image of a disappointed God, inevitably recall his father. Three years earlier, during that first pretrial hearing, the reporter Sam Stanton had peered over the elder Ben Williams's shoulder as the courtroom listened to the scratchy recording of his wife's initial prison conversation with their son. Stanton told me how he'd seen the old man taking notes on three-by-five cards. "No critical thinking!" he wrote energetically, marking the exclamation point with a punch. Exactly like his son, he was an unforgiving judge.

Now more than ever, Ben experienced loneliness, disregard, and hopelessness. His world was his cell. The painted cinder-block walls, the ledge of a bed spanning the whole cell's width, another ledge for a table, a fluorescent light fixture with no on/off switch, a stainless steel console with a tiny sink on top and a seatless toilet angled from the corner. That was it. The prowler started bringing him Klonopin (clonazepam), a sometimes habit-forming anti-anxiety medication.

The attack on Renault was an open-and-shut case. The state got the entire arrest/trial/conviction out of the way before the Matson and Mowder capital murder case even began. On Halloween, October 31, 2002, Ben was convicted of the attempted murder of Timothy Renault. He was due to be sentenced December 2 and was facing life in prison. He'd already gotten thirty years for arson in federal court. The Matson and Mowder trial was scheduled to begin December 10. In that one, Ben was facing death.

Now Ben becomes invisible for a moment as if a crucial scene's been snipped out. Who knows what he was thinking? It's tempting to imagine a sense of responsibility was beginning to leak through the massive dikes of his mind. But it's easier to believe his agony was as uncomprehending as ever. A kind of ecstatic self-pity. For the purposes of a story he needs to come to, wake up at least for a moment. But sometimes a splendid pointlessness floods imagined constructs like stories. Nothing ends the right way. We just back off. The protagonist comes to appear as small and mute as a guppy struggling on the floor beside its tank. History or Story are overwhelmed by the eternal drone of Nature.

Ben was about to undergo some tests—a brain scan,

among others—in connection with his defense in the upcoming Matson and Mowder trial, though he can't have
felt there was much point in any defense now. For the brain
scan he was abruptly ordered off Klonopin on November 7.
Withdrawal from Klonopin can be hard for some people,
but Ben had nine days to adjust.

Happiness almost always feels contingent or tentative,
but despair carries a kind of certitude, even if you try to
tell yourself it's only a chemical thing (not the kind of re-
assurance that would have occurred to Ben Williams anyway). November 16 was a Saturday. Ben spent the evening
reading the Bible in bed. He was last observed at one thirty
a.m. When he set his Bible on the ledge table, he left it
open to the 22nd Psalm, the most abject of all the Psalms
of David:

> My God, my God, why hast thou forsaken me? . . .
> But I am a worm, and no man;
> a reproach of men, and despised of the people.
> All they that see me laugh me to scorn:
> they shoot out the lip, they shake the head saying,
> He trusted on the LORD that he would deliver him:
> let him deliver him, seeing he delighted in him . . .

Ben had crafted his last tool. He'd broken the flexible
blade from a plastic razor. He remounted it with string
between a pair of ballpoint pen refills. Because it was hard
to handle, he tied the blade to his wrist to give it traction
for cutting.

He was naked except for the jail-issue tangerine briefs.
I imagine he was so inclined to nakedness because our natural state reminded him of Eden. He wore an amulet on

dental floss around his neck, a silver dollar–sized package of tin foil containing two Bible verses, a seed, a tiny piece of soap, and a crumb of chocolate.

He stuffed cardboard under the cell door. He spread his blanket behind the stainless steel sink/toilet console. He sat on the floor with his back against it—the only place in the cell where you were a little hidden from the window. He cut himself, beginning with his arm, leg, or neck—who knows?

The blade was hard to manipulate. It was narrow. It wasn't easy to cut deeply. He seems to have made several attempts to get at the carotid artery in his neck, but muscle and tendon probably writhed under the pressure of the blade. He drew long slices up his arm. The surface veins bled for a while, but the flow kept trailing off. He may have cut himself twenty or thirty times by now. He'd lost a lot of blood. He would be cold, trembling with chills, queasy, dizzy. He would be starting to go into shock. But he was still awake.

It's impossible to know if any thoughts or images broke through. Does a suicide grieve for himself or the world? Here he was, naked and covered in sticky blood again, his own this time, not Renault's. Was that a kind of atonement? Was this punishment or self-sacrifice?

Soon he'd cut himself forty or fifty times. Because he was in shock and the nerves of his skin were starved for blood, the cutting likely hurt much less. He pressed an inch deep where he could, but he was trembling badly. He kept at it.

Maybe it came down to stubbornness. Suicide, too, was a matter of honor. He wasn't going to fail at this. He couldn't. How would it look to his father and the world?

Far from meaning he was sorry for his life, this was the only way to prove he'd been serious all along. He wasn't going to fail. He kept cutting. Around the seventy-fifth cut he managed to sever an artery. The blood poured out to the rhythm of his heartbeat, which soon abated and eventually came to a feathery stop.

DA McGregor Scott, who viewed the lacerated, marble-white body after it was discovered at six thirty in the morning, was reminded of what he'd read of the bodies found at Little Bighorn. After battle, Indians mutilated the bodies of their enemies so they couldn't pursue them, or continue fighting, in the afterlife. Ben's suicide had everything to do with this life, however—like they all do. He'd ended the ultimate argument by torturing himself to death. Probably not from guilt so much as in a last magniloquent refusal to be proved wrong.

3
BAD-GOOD, NOT GOOD

The idea of "hate crimes" makes me uncomfortable, because admitting "hate crimes" looks like criminalizing motive, and that looks like criminalizing thought. This observation may be too purely logical for the real world, where we're constantly forced to make messy political adjustments so that society will work a little better than it has in the past. Maybe the idea of "hate crimes" is needed to make hatred and cruelty socially visible. And maybe the concept won't ever entail punishable thought.

After withering in committee for years beginning in 2001, the Matthew Shepard and James Byrd Jr. Hate Crimes Prevention Act was finally passed by the House and Senate and signed into law in 2009. A prominent politician told me that the law ought to have been called the Matson and Mowder Act, because the two California men *really* never did anything to justify what happened to them. I'm certain the politician didn't mean to imply that Matthew Shepard deserved to be murdered because *maybe* he tried to pick up some guys or *maybe* he took meth and the whole thing was a drug deal gone bad. Still, the words came out without a second thought.

A similar problem dogs many of the crimes I've looked at. The murdered man is older. He's gay. He may be paying for sex. He may look like a pervert or a predator or a low-life. Maybe he is one. Either way, it's hard to think of him as a victim. We like our victims to be as pure as new-fallen snow, like Matson and Mowder. Indeed, the "gay panic defense" was designed to make killers look like good boys in comparison to their victims, but the truth is, good boys don't kill. (Usually. Later on it'll become clear this doesn't always hold with gangs of boys.)

I used to wonder about the silly Shangri-Las lyric "He's good-bad, but he's not evil." Sung/spoken with dotty sincerity, the phrase seems to encapsulate Americans' fond indulgence for the bullying and cruelty of boys. We have to do something to domesticate those perfectly ordinary and human traits—comedy, military discipline, sports—but what better, more magical solution than to use the power of love to turn them *cute*?

I believe Ben Williams thought he was cute. I'm not talking about looks. Unfortunately, if aggression, domination, violence aren't cute, they can undoubtedly be fun. This gets complicated. I knew a muscle-bound doorman at a famous nightclub who loved nothing better than to gay-bash in his off hours. It didn't matter that he was secretly gay himself or that his relationship with his boyfriend was a competition to see who could get bigger through steroids and "top" the other. Yet the violence wasn't merely self-hatred. Gay people prowling for sex at night happened to be available and vulnerable. And violence was exhilarating, even joyful.

It was disconcerting that this friend looked into my eyes once and told me, "You get it," because I've always thought of myself as the least violent person in the world. I didn't grow up with it. I never had cartoon fantasies about it. If anything, I was afraid of pain and averse to competition. I was masculine enough—in the self-repressed way—

to avoid being bullied growing up. Beyond that, nothing special. But where was the violence in me beyond the occasional slammed door?—because, of course, my friend was right in some way, since here I am working on this book. Maybe I was bad-good, not good. Not as deluded as Ben Williams, of course, but maybe a thread of subtle cruelty ran through my decency. In fact, I do recall an instance or two when I bullied someone as a kid, both with a group of other boys and alone. And, though gay, I'm "average" enough to find the foibles of gay people laughable under the right circumstances, just like anyone else.

On the other hand, I see myself in the victims of these murders. Many of them were bad-good in a different way— say, good enough, but dirty. And I? A trashy bar holds no mystery for me. I shrug about sexual behavior some people find shocking. I laugh at things others hold sacred. I have a fondness for lowlife. So I would be what many people consider bad, until I'm murdered by someone worse, which would make me a little good in retrospect. Bad-good. But, really, what am I?

The case I write about next turned out to be more personal than I expected. That's why I put "I" into it more than before, and why I've just tied myself in knots. I knew I'd get mixed up talking about bad and good here and, in fact, I meant to. I wanted to illustrate a habit of thought typical of fretful young men by demonstrating it. This is what happens when paradoxes and simplistic dualities battle it out in our minds. It's an abstract struggle, a battle between forces like *womanly and manly* or *top and bottom* or *alpha and omega* or *winner and loser* or, of course, *good and bad*, even among all of them at once, and the struggle usually plays out with infinitely more intensity than I've shown above. Violence comes into it. Young men project this purely personal psychological effort to order their experience of the world *onto* the real world. With the energy of youth, they take desperate measures to make the simplistic real. Describing their actions as "hate crimes" isn't sufficient, nor does this term take into account the terrible joy of violence.

4
DOMER, QUALLS, AND MADDEN, 2007

I. *Nervous*

Afterward people said Bradley Qualls was tweaking, a meth head in a rut. He was overwrought, at any rate, and maybe he was rubbing his shaved head the way an addict will, seven, eight times, using the same tensed-up spiral stroke each time. But people were wrong. He wasn't on meth. Since joining Chaos Squad he'd gotten straight. Skinhead rules were strict about that. Watching him, Darrell Madden, a so-called "general" in Chaos Squad, couldn't keep near-hallucinatory suspicion from building inside him: the younger, bigger Qualls looked like he was losing control. (Again! The day after the murder he'd taken Darrell's gun and threatened to kill himself.) Really, they were both losing control. Three or four visits to the body and it still felt unreal. How the hell hadn't the body been found yet? The missing man was all over TV. They were losing it, but Darrell was better at faking calm—better at faking anything. Even as a kid Brad was wild, mouthy, uncontrollable, authentic. Darrell was a compulsive actor. Now, years later, in prison, Darrell keeps repeating to me: everything was about control.

They were in Ardmore, Oklahoma, halfway between Oklahoma City and Dallas–Ft. Worth. Darrell's girlfriend had dropped them off at the Huntington Falls Apartments, a little collection of ecru townhomes and too-empty parking lots off Sam Noble Parkway. Brad's girlfriend rented here.

In a sham, '80s way, the two-story townhomes looked tonier than they really were. Under the development's name was a discreet blue equal-opportunity sign, but black and white underclasses mixed uneasily here. The inflexible racial divide that exists in prison seemed to echo out here. African American residents hated crossing paths with Bradley Qualls or, much worse, his new friend Darrell, a slight, pallid, smirking skinhead whose neck was ringed by thick black tattoos, including SS bolts and some phrase in *deutsche Schrift*. Their worst fears would've been confirmed had Darrell ever removed his shirt to show off the Nazi eagle and *God's Grace Is the White Race* across his chest. Or the swastika on his shoulder. Jug-eared, green-eyed, he looked a lot younger than thirty-seven. He was a genuine skinhead, the bad kind, though the line of stubble on his scalp showed he'd been balding since before he shaved his head. Maybe vanity played a part along with the politics.

Bradley was twenty-six. He couldn't quite pull off the Aryan skinhead look. His scalp's stubble was dense and black. His soul patch was too long, a satanic tongue. Plus his skin was dark, less Nordic, more Native American– or Mexican-looking. His eyes drooped at their outer corners. He looked like any snickering pot-smoker, any sleepy Oklahoma loser. Before his stint at Dick Connor Correctional Center in Hominy in 2001, he'd grown up listening to rap music. The friends he had, the few kids who didn't tease him mercilessly about being in special education, were all black. Now everything was different.

Just yesterday, Brad had had the words *skin head* tattooed on his face, exactly like Darrell. Brad's momentous tattoo—wasn't he trying to become Darrell in a way?—caused a staph infection. One was popping up on Darrell's arm as well, and Darrell knew how bad they could get. Paranoid about that, he had his girlfriend take them both to the hospital. Brad's mother Tina Melton came and picked Brad up. The infected spot on his face was still ruddy and swollen now. Maybe the antibiotics were making him hyper.

In truth, Brad was a lot more volatile than Darrell, something Darrell resented. He hated being outdone even in a fault. Darrell was the leader, the general. But Brad, a kid, a raw recruit, had a directionless masculine anger, hair-trigger and intimidating. Once, his sister Michelle recalls wryly, wearing only his underwear, he'd chased her worthless husband down the street brandishing a toilet plunger.

On this day Brad and Darrell were arguing. According to Darrell, Brad kept saying he'd never snitched before. That was why they'd sent him to Dick Connor just for stealing car stereos: he wouldn't snitch. But trust wasn't in Darrell's nature. And right now, the last thing he wanted was to let things get out of hand again the way they had the night of the killing. Even fake calm was fine. A few days ago he'd told Brad it was okay to smoke some weed, not strictly allowed under skinhead rules. Maybe Brad had snuck something again today. Ever since going off Ritalin, Adderall, the works, at fourteen, Brad had used pot like medicine. His whole life he'd needed to be turned down a few notches.

A cop says Chaos Squad was a "gang of two." Darrell hints at a whole shadowy world of members, rules, and ranks. ("A DISorganization," he allows.) Certainly Brad, a bare few months ago, excitedly told his sister Michelle that he was going to meet "the leader." And they were gang enough for the FBI to get involved later. Who exactly came to Darrell's Chaos Squad tattoo parties—recruits, soldiers, bored Oklahoman riffraff? It depends on who's talking, but you can picture it. Drawling, half-dressed, embittered kids straggle into the crash pad in Ardmore, the tattoo parlor in Edmond, or Darrell's own trailer in Washington. The buzzing tattoo gun slowly draws SS bolts or Hitler's birth date in navy ink flecked with blood. Letters and figures gleam darkly from inflamed halos on pale greenish skin.

Darrell had been sober, no drugs, for over two years. He'd taken only antidepressants since he got out of Jess Dunn Correctional Center after fifteen months, himself freshly tattooed Chaos Squad–style. He'd done stints at Crabtree and back in California, but now he really looked like an ex-con. Eyebrows (Brad's model; when shaved, they read: *skin head*), ankle, arms, neck, chest, back. (Maybe he was hoping that labeling his body permanently and on the inside would establish once and for all who he was. After so many years of deception, it didn't work. He was still continually falling through one self into another. Some days he couldn't remember which name he was using until someone spoke to him. Billy, Lynn, Richie Rich. Never "Darrell." Only his family called him that.) Yet he says Chaos rules, oxymoron or not, had been good. They'd kept him sober. You could deal, not use. It was a big change from three years ago: strung out in Mexico, weighing 130 pounds at most.

The word was getting out. People were learning what Darrell and Brad had done. When you overheard two jittery skinheads, half-cocky, half-spooked, talking about how they'd killed some guy, you didn't go, "Oh, really? Tell me about it." You said nothing at first. You asked nothing. But people did overhear. Eventually they started talking.

What Brad and Darrell had done was catching up with them. Despite their brutal jokes about a man so passive he wouldn't fight for his own life, despite their wild plans to kill the people who overheard them talking or who knew too much, they must have felt a demonic weariness. Brad was spinning out of control. Darrell, too, was at the breaking point, though he was unaware of it. Perhaps he could only experience small, locket-sized measures of feeling like the ones an actor draws on when playing a character ostensibly unlike himself. Darrell's many explosive yet eerily playful "acts" of violence and hatred had always seemed well performed in the sense that their author was drawing on something real but also small and remote within himself. However wild he was, a nonactor like Brad would have now *felt* he was a killer more intensely than Darrell ever could. A sense of shunned doom would have haunted him.

Though Chaos rules said you could never talk, Darrell himself boasted on the Chaos Squad MySpace page that he'd killed a woman once (he tells me now he's murdered several times but confides that this claim wasn't true; the group was simply trying to scare somebody). After the real killing he wrote on MySpace that "the juice in the needle" was likely to get him because of something that had happened. It was hard not to talk. The very day after the murder, Brad's mother, Tina Melton, all innocence, had come over to Darrell's trailer for Jack Daniel's and beer, an impromptu sort of party, incredibly enough. The girlfriends were there too. During the night Brad told his mom what had happened. Later Brad fought with his girlfriend, stole Darrell's gun, and threatened to kill himself.

Darrell blew up the next day: "You told your mom about what happened?" He says Brad shouted back, "I told you she was cool! I told you she was cool!" Trying to impose Chaos rules, Darrell ordered Brad to send Tina Melton an e-mail telling her to pay no attention to what she'd heard the night before. And Brad had done it. Darrell stood over him and watched as he typed the e-mail. Still, something wild, disobedient, and, of course, genuinely murderous about Brad was already starting to spook Darrell.

At some point that day—the day of the big argument—Brad called his sister Michelle. He pleaded with her, "Can I come over to Grandma's? I want to see Mom . . . I just need to come over!" For whatever reason Michelle turned him down, and Brad got angry at her. Listening in, Darrell thought that was just as well. He wasn't going to let Brad out of his sight in the state he was in. The two had stopped by to see Michelle a few days earlier and Darrell could tell she realized something was up. Brad wouldn't look at her. He'd hung his head. He'd hugged her kids with valedictory, bearlike passion.

Now, at the Huntington Falls Apartments, the argument got worse. A witness later told a reporter, "Brad was kind of tweaking . . . you could tell he was on something. The other guy was saying, *You need to calm down*." According to Darrell, Brad had started saying he thought he could lead Chaos Squad if he wanted.

Suspicion was becoming a kind of delirium in Darrell. For a while already he'd felt certain Brad was working up his courage to call the police. Anxiety about his own colossal deceptions was plaguing him. He claims Brad had been hinting about turning himself in for more than a week. Brad, he says, would come out with things like, "You saw the news, man. You think they don't know it was us already? I'll take the fall. I can do it. I never snitched." Released from Dick Connor in 2006 after five years, he thought he knew what to expect. From prison now, Darrell mentions this condescendingly and adds, "You could tell this was the first time he killed somebody." It doesn't seem to have occurred to Darrell that Brad's wanting to turn himself in, or wanting to kill himself, may have represented a kind of moral exhaustion or, even, remorse. When he first tells me the story, Darrell explains that the reason Brad wanted to kill himself was because he'd fought with his girlfriend. When I suggest that murdering someone the night before might have had something to do with it, Darrell thinks about that a moment and then agrees, but with a real sense of surprise as if the idea had never dawned on him.

The line about taking over Chaos Squad was new. "I'm not sure if I misunderstood what he was saying," Darrell tells me now. They crossed the Huntington Falls Apartments parking lot. The breeze or a confused, novel sense of alarm caused a chill to ripple forward across Darrell's scalp. It was November 7. Though there'd been a bit of a heat wave around Amarillo and up into the panhandle that month, today was cool, midsixties. They wore jackets. Darrell's was hanging over the lump of the gun in his shoulder holster. They climbed the stairs to the apartment.

At five o'clock in early November the sun is low. A few long cirrus clouds look accidental, as if a painter has fallen off his ladder. A minor rush hour takes place on the main roads, but here the parking lot and streets are dead quiet. More like a Saturday than a Wednesday afternoon. Loosely strung wire on creosoted pine telephone poles cast scalloped shadows on L Street and Sam Noble Parkway.

From the second-story apartment landing the western sky is so immense the town below looks two-dimensional in comparison. Lampposts and flagpoles prick up hopelessly. Ardmore's inevitable strip-mall-scape is suffused with the childish and intense boredom that is something of an American national characteristic, like quaintness in the Alps or grandeur in Paris.

As if completely blind to the world, forever emitting, never absorbing, Brad blustered on, according to Darrell. Even as they entered the apartment they were arguing. This is when Brad said the words Darrell particularly remembers, the ones he says made him snap: "I am Chaos Squad."

Darrell was focused on himself, keenly aware that he was smaller physically, worried about returning to prison. Now, suddenly, like Proteus, the control issue came up in an ungraspable new form. They entered Brad's girlfriend's apartment. She was sitting on the couch. Her kid was playing in the next room.

It happened in a moment, like the chill crawling over his naked scalp. Darrell envisioned Brad yapping to his girlfriend, to his mom, to his sister, to the police, to whomever and whatever Chaos Squad really was, and the ice gave way: he fell into his deepest self. He lived with the chill from this personality but was hardly ever *in* it. Maybe it was something too deep to call a "self."

A few thoughts played on the surface far above him: if Brad turned himself in he was going to make a deal, basically snitch. Brad—this mess of a guy he didn't even know that well—had a plan. He was going to take his general down. Hadn't he been laying it out over the past few days? Maybe he meant to make a deal and then try to take over Chaos Squad. Darrell shook his gun loose from the holster.

Brad turned. Like an angry, gape-mouthed bear, he looked oddly dainty as if he were going to hop or stamp his feet. Darrell shot him in the shoulder. Darrell's mind drifted across one of those curious prairies of stopped time. As if there were no rush at all, he calculated: twenty-five years for that shot alone—the other murder comes out, could be life—what the hell? He shot Brad three more times in the chest.

The kid started making noise in the next room. The body dropped like a sandbag on its left side, its head resting against the couch next to the girlfriend. Darrell is certain the girl thought that this was some kind of fake gunplay—that they were trying to freak her out. It took a long moment for a look of dreadful stupidity to cross her face. Blood was everywhere.

People in the area, living with that faint echo of prison society, naturally recognized gunshots. A door opened. A screen door squealed. Darrell picked up his bag containing another clip and two hundred extra rounds and backed out the apartment door. He trotted downstairs but slowed to a fast walk. A black woman in a do-rag saw him with the gun. After steadying herself against the apartment complex's playground fence, she clutched her head crying, "Oh my God! Oh my God!" Darrell jammed the gun in his shoulder holster. He flinched when he brushed the hot tip of the muzzle across his T-shirt. Once he got down the grassy embankment to Sam Noble Parkway, he headed west into the grid of Ardmore's residential streets, still at a walk. He avoided the huge Valero oil refinery directly north.

He zigzagged but kept heading west and a little north. It must have felt strange walking through that small-town neighborhood, quarter-acre lots and not-very-old two- and three-bedroom houses. Kids were on the street. Here was a man waxing his car. Since Darrell was trying to get on the road—whether by carjack, home invasion, or robbery—he paused to bum a cigarette off the man. (He doesn't smoke.) You can almost taste the man's luck, not smoky, but a flavor as clean and startling as snow. It's hard to believe thoughts as intense as this weren't visible: "I changed my mind at the last minute. I was afraid he would resist and I would have to shoot him." Darrell kept walking.

The sky had begun to darken. But Darrell was only on the north side of town, near the big intersection of North Commerce and Veteran's Boulevard, where traffic lazed to a stop and yawned back into motion. A low gray Skateland building sprawled on one corner. They'd tried to dress it up with a sad, tidy row of trimmed bushes. Across from a huge vacant lot, aluminum streetlights were coming on with that staticky noise—like a monocular alien clearing its throat. A City of Ardmore police cruiser glided up beside Darrell. Spooked, he took off into the street. The cruiser stopped in the middle of the intersection, lights revolving.

The lines of cars came to a synchronized, rocking-horse stop. Frowning moon faces leaned into side windows. The frowns vanished when Darrell took out his gun. His free hand scrabbled at flush door handles. He couldn't tell if he was shouting. The cars sped up like frightened cows. They started streaming between Darrell and the cruiser. Everyone was terrified. Out of pure desperation Darrell took a potshot at the trunk of one car. He pointed the gun at a guy in a pickup.

By now, the Ardmore cop, Josh McGee, an African American, was out of his own car. Darrell swung the gun toward him thinking that would keep him at bay. He remembers saying something like, "Go away! Leave me alone and no one will get hurt." He felt a blow, like a fist, to his upper left arm, and for an instant imagined that the cop, who'd been more than halfway across the street, had somehow punched him, until he realized he'd been shot. He felt the downbeat of pain and dizziness. No longer under his own control, his body crumpled before he was able to run a step.

Meanwhile, Brad's sister Michelle got a call on her cell phone from a friend at the Huntington Falls Apartments. She remembers hearing, "How come y'all aren't down here? You know, Brad's been shot, and I gotta tell you the ambulance was already here and they left without him." What that meant didn't register. Michelle hurried over. As soon as she arrived people pointed her out to the cops. "That's Qualls's sister." The cops stopped her and kept demanding, "Where's Madden? Where's Darrell Madden?" Who? She had no idea who they wanted. She knew him by a different name and finally got out, "Richie? I don't know." When the police wouldn't let her into the apartment, she put it together. She sank to her knees.

Michelle got on the phone to her mom. Tina Melton and her husband jumped in their car and sped over to the apartments. Along the way, they had to crawl through the intersection of North Commerce and Veteran's Boulevard, partially blocked by police cruisers. Over the phone Michelle could hear her mother Tina screaming at her father, "Is that that son of a bitch?" Then: "Michelle, they got him in handcuffs and there's blood all over the place." Michelle heard her father's voice rumble. She heard Tina shout again, "Stop the car! Let me out of this car! Is that the motherfucker? There's blood all over the place!" Michelle's father didn't stop.

* * *

The bullet in Darrell's arm eventually needed seven surgeries to repair, not exactly the easy, debonair wound of old movies. His radial nerve had been severed, so Darrell would lose the ability to raise his wrist or spread his fingers. He now jokes that the limp wrist is "poetic justice, right?" They moved him to a hospital in Oklahoma City where he was surely the least-loved patient.

Thursday he didn't remember. Friday he wasn't allowed to eat. Supposedly, you couldn't have food for twenty-four hours before an operation, but Darrell doubted they were much concerned about him.

Two OKC cops were posted outside his door. With a jailbird's punctiliousness about the rules, Darrell knew they weren't allowed to come into the room. Of course, they did, he claims. The black cop smiled at the slip of an ailing skinhead inked all over with racist and Nazi crap. According to Darrell, the two officers switched the channel to Black Entertainment Television and exchanged shit-eating grins. They ragged on him. Darrell kicked at his leg restraints. He threw the remote and caught the white guy on the lip. This is Darrell's version of events, naturally.

The cops happily grabbed at their belts for Tasers. One tased him on the rib cage, one on the neck. The Tasers work for five seconds. Then you have to press the button and shoot again. Darrell claims it happened at least three times. Fans of tendon and muscle popped out under his jaw. He pissed himself.

The next day, after he came out of the first surgery, they let him eat. They served spaghetti. When Darrell hollered for a fork, a cop came in and told him he couldn't have any plastic. The cop didn't say another word but appeared to find Darrell's bitching the most entertaining thing in the world. He waited until Darrell realized there was no option but to eat the spaghetti with his fingers. Darrell didn't eat that night, until a black nurse brought him some packages of saltines, a kindness he remembers to this day. For myself, I can't help wondering what she was thinking when she looked at him. *God's Grace Is the White Race.* If only *her* thoughts had been visible!

It wasn't something that showed, but Darrell had given up on everything. No hope for the next minute, nor for the rest of his life. He had moods left, anger mostly, but that was all. Because the anger was, in a way, absolute, true, not an act; it felt almost good, powerful at any rate. He seized the plastic piss-pot half full of urine and threw it at the cop. This one, he claims, nearly emptied a can of pepper spray on him. Darrell was charged with assaulting a police officer.

Six days later FBI agents came to interview him. Because they, at least, behaved respectfully, Darrell says, he told them almost everything.

It's hard to square the different images I have. Reading newspaper accounts of the murders, I note that reporters haven't gone much beyond "skinhead" in their character-izations. Like a lazy casting director, I've first conjured up a certain Germanic/Slavic physical type, a particular sneer-ing attitude. But the age is off. Thirty-seven is too old. It's easy to understand the reporters' heavy sarcasm in calling Darrell a "self-described general." The title is absurd, more than a little pompous. I've found a series of pictures of Dar-rell, past prison ID photos, front, back, and sides. He ages a little across the series, the shaved hairline recedes, he puts on a few more pounds and many more tattoos, including the notorious teardrop on his cheek, but he doesn't look scary enough. He wears a slight smirk. His close-set eyes are mild. This skinhead (and, to hear him tell it, multiple murderer already) has an air of irony, an uncertain smart-aleck affect that seems out of place in an inmate you expect to be an indifferent lump or a human jack-o'-lantern along the lines of the pathetically performative Charles Manson.

I've also watched extensive film of Darrell at around age twenty. He's a different person altogether. Mop-haired, he appears preppy, a pretty-boy clothing-store associate in New York or LA. He's extremely well spoken—no trace of a countrified or Oklahoma accent.

Even now, Darrell's writing (we've exchanged letters for over two years) is what used to be called "girl writing," plump printing crossed with the Palmer method, little round circles dotting the i's. (Looking back, I see he made the first few letters appear more "butch.") If, having grown up on TV and mystery stories, I know that anyone can be the murderer, I find it almost impossible to imagine this person throwing a punch, surviving in prison, flying into rages, or captivating and seducing more stereotypical skinheads. Apparently he did.

I've seen footage of him emerging from the courtroom (after weeping at his trial for the first murder). He looks like an embarrassed, if aged-out high school kid as he ignores a reporter shouting, "Is it true you lived with a man? Why did you do it if you're gay yourself?" On the surface, or at that particular moment, the reporter is the unpleasant one, not the guy in shackles and an orange jumpsuit. So be it. It's the duty of unreflective local TV news reporters to be the loudmouthed voice of their community. Anyway, morality and pleasantness aren't identical, which brings me to the final and most challenging detail to be incorporated in the portrait. When I meet Darrell, I like him instantly. He has a subtle but potent charisma that works backward, making you feel like the brilliant or fascinating one. I lie on the bed of my cheap Oklahoma City motel room (smoking, please) and second-guess for hours my sense of comfort and companionability with the killer I've just met.

In a tone reminiscent of Elizabethan broadsheets like *The Ordinary of Newgate, his account of the behaviour, confession, and dying words, of the malefactors, who were executed at Tyburn, etc.* . . . the *Daily Ardmoreite* reported on Darrell's first guilty plea:

> *Darrell Madden's tough-guy Skinhead persona dissolved into tears and trembling Friday as he pleaded guilty to murdering Bradley Qualls Nov. 7 and his subsequent attempts to carjack a getaway vehicle in northwest Ardmore. Madden's performance raised the question: was this a single dramatic display or a rehearsal for the additional charges he now faces in Oklahoma County for the torture-murder of an Edmond man? Several times during his court appearance Friday in front of Associate District Judge Lee Card, Madden collapsed on the defendant's table in a flood of tears and wails.*

Is this really an accurate account? I have as hard a time picturing these outbursts as I do picturing some of Darrell's other exploits: killing six llamas in a rage, coolly impersonating a police officer. Maybe the reporter was right to suspect an act.

Darrell has told me he's seen psychiatrists most of his life. "I have been on all kinds of mental health drugs for many reasons, but the only real mental problems I have had [were] depression and bulimia as an adult." In another list of his diagnoses he mentions "psychotic tendencies" as if that had been part of a report of some kind. One of his letters to me explains:

> As a child I had ADD, ADHD. But as far as hearing voices and them telling me what to do or anything, I have not. I have lied saying that I had in the past, to get the drugs and to get money from the state and the government . . . I am pretty close to normal, kind of ☺! As far as suicide . . . Mostly for attention.

Elsewhere he's mentioned seven suicide attempts.

In truth, the first time he listed his mental problems for me, I reacted with impatience. None of it makes him "innocent," and neither liking nor compassion is any argument that a killer is less of a killer.

During the day I drive a rented car all over south-central Oklahoma and a bit of north Texas looking at the disappointingly ordinary locations of the "story." I take a lot of pictures, but I could be anywhere. The drama has beaded up and trickled away like desert rain. Nothing evocative stirs at the An-Son car wash either, back in Oklahoma City, where Brad and Darrell met the man Darrell now calls "Mr. Domer"—strangely, but how do you address someone you've murdered? Mr. Domer and Darrell are joined forever, and neither has anything to say about it now. "I've done such really awful, awful things," Darrell says, in a tone too ambiguous to be satisfying. He means to be remorseful, but in the end, it's just an observation.

The effort of imagination and second-guessing takes more of a toll than I expected. I allow myself one moment of leisure during my visit to Oklahoma City. I go to the

Museum of Osteology, a tidy warehouse with a spectacular collection of skeletons. It may seem a strange choice to clear my head when dreaming about two horrible murders day and night, but the illusion of order in the museum is satisfying. Here, death is put to good use. Here, all the animals are white stick figures, mouse to marmot to giraffe. The pristine display cases are a 3-D flipbook of obvious homologies, an eternal unity across changes in form. But a sign in the primate case warning that the museum doesn't mean to endorse evolution causes a feeling of betrayal. Oklahoma is a foreign country to me.

II. *Wild*

October 26, 2007 was the last Friday before Halloween, so people came out in all sorts of costumes, and the stretch of NW 39th Street in Oklahoma City, the walkable and hard-drinking "gay neighborhood," was busy—considering this is a state where "gay" hardly exists, a state where all the porn is soft and go-go girls and boys are required by law to keep their thongs in place. The bars regularly hired security guards to keep an eye out for gay-bashers and religious protesters, though tonight security at Tramps and Angles had its hands full carding everyone to keep out the underage.

On the corner of North Barnes, across from the parking lot for Tramps, the notorious An-Son car wash was busy too, in its dim, surreptitious way. That was the hustlers' hangout. The quiet hum of commerce and romance on the street kept being interrupted by musical blasts when club doors opened, by distant car alarms, by squalls of acrobatic laughter, and by the occasional ecstatic hoot—half-queen, half-cowboy. Despite the noise, and though you were in the middle of a decent-sized city, a pointed absence of sound was also easy to make out as the encompassing loneliness of the Osage Plains.

Darrell got Brad to wear a tight T-shirt and camo ripped just so to show a little thigh on both sides. He dressed the same way himself. Maybe not quite as showy, because . . . how would it look if it appeared like he knew what he was doing? ("I told Brad this was how we rolled queers in LA. He had no reason to doubt me. Little did he know.") Like the next card in blackjack, everything Darrell kept hidden about himself must have felt *this close* to being revealed. He remembers thinking Brad, the Chaos Squad prospect, was so wired he'd scare people off. Even dressed up, Brad was too intimidating and too straight-seeming to pass.

They started at about nine o'clock. They walked the eighteen miles from Washington to the gay area in downtown Oklahoma City. It took them several footsore hours. Since the route takes almost an hour by car, I thought it possible they were dropped off and that Darrell was telling me he walked the route to protect someone else. When I mentioned that "someone unknown" may have driven them, Darrell answered, "We got one ride that entire trip. Only one . . . I kept forgetting where I was going. It all looked very different on foot and took a very, very long time." For the purposes of this crime anyway, they were a gang of two. They spent the walk reviewing exactly how the evening would go, what they'd do, how they'd act. The plan itself had been settled the previous night before going to bed. Darrell describes their long conversation as a boastful amalgam of quasimilitary planning and gruesome fantasy.

Once they arrived at that corner of Barnes, they sat on a low, pale brick wall by the An-Son car wash. Darrell knew how to do this: act friendly yet as deliberate as a house cat gazing into a guest's eyes. The shaved head didn't feel like the great disguise it actually was. He was afraid of being recognized. Some people gave them a wide berth. Drivers slowed. Gazes snagged on them, slid down their bodies, and were nervously yanked loose.

Two older men passed slowly in a new Lexus. They circled the block a few times. Darrell watched them murmuring in the dashboard light. The driver shook his head at his bald friend. Later, the driver, a closeted man who had to be subpoenaed to testify (social pressure in Oklahoma makes the plains air feel as thick as a jungle's), said that he'd gotten a bad vibe from the two skinheads. He didn't like the tattoos. Consider how well known it is that the teardrop stands for a murder.[4] But the bald man, for whatever reason, was interested. Maybe a few drinks or Halloween giddiness made him more daring than usual, or maybe he was unconcerned because he wasn't carrying enough cash to matter if he were robbed. Besides, Darrell is slight. I find him unintimidating myself. Also, Darrell had finally decided Brad should wait around a corner because he just didn't look right, so the scarier of the skinheads was gone later. The two older men, Quentin and Steve, had eaten dinner together and drove back to Quentin's place. Quentin says Steve stopped just long enough to run to the bathroom and was off. Now, driving his own new (preowned) Mercury, Steve made a beeline to the An-Son car wash and cruised past Darrell once more. He gave the familiar nod.

---

4. According to Darrell, it's more complicated than I realize. "It all depends on which side it is on and even on the color. On the left side it means 'in memory' of someone who has died and is always done in black ink either lined or filled in. On the right side it means that you have killed someone. It can be lined or filled in black. When it is red and black-lined it means that it is 'wet' and that you have killed in the name [of], or for, your gang." Darrell's teardrop is on the right side, red, black-lined—wet.

Steven Domer was a sixty-two-year-old bachelor who lived in Edmond with his divorced older brother. Bald as a cue ball, he wore a bushy walrus mustache and had the still-in-good-shape bearing of a Romanian Olympic coach. Blink your eyes and you could see a different person through the masculine image, a man with a gentle, brown-eyed enthusiasm, hungry for company, generous to a fault. He wore a white T-shirt and a small trickle of gold around his neck.

Steve Domer came from a background of violence. According to Mort, Steve's brother, their father was quick to anger, brutal, and often scornful of his younger son. Steve never reconciled with him. Reputedly, the father had had a taste for boys, and after he died in an automobile accident in '74, the family minister refused to conduct his funeral. A stranger preached a eulogy whose bland untruth nearly caused Steve to fall out of the pew. That was in Ft. Wayne, Indiana, the family's original home. Mort recounts all this with the simple honesty he promised me at the beginning of our conversation.

Steve had left home by the time his father died. Bearded and long-haired, he and that year's boyfriend (the boyfriends never lasted) headed for San Francisco. The car made it as far as Oklahoma City where it broke down. Steve chose to make his life here. He ran through much younger boyfriends like clockwork, probably only half-aware that his paying for beauty school, for one example, figured into it as much as love. He liked to play the helpful swain to elderly neighbors. He was a near-obsessive collector of stuff. Never-worn shoes and T-shirts piled up in his Edmond house along with ceramic *objets d'art* and ornaments from his years working at United Design, a "giftware/collectibles" manufacturer. He had his vanities. He liked to hint that he came from money and kept Mort in the background when necessary. He attended First Presbyterian, the church of local grandees like the Braums. He hated getting older and wasn't above using a bit of cover-up on the dark circles under his eyes. Even if his boyfriends were lowlifes, even if he'd dabbled in dealing marijuana when he first moved to town, he had a nice house and had made it a long way from his father's violent anger. (Though knowing how to survive violence could have made him a little bolder about taking risks later.)

Violence requires a certain education. Macho folklore advises you to get into at least one fistfight when young to avoid turning into a physical coward. Supposedly a ninth-century knight would plunge his little son's hands into the gore of a slain enemy to inoculate the kid against the horror of violent death. Disproportionate numbers of butchers, inured to slaughter, become murderers, according to anecdote. But nowadays many, if not most, men are practically illiterate when it comes to violence. (It doesn't seem to be required to get and wield real power in the modern world. Just the opposite, perhaps.) But like Steve Domer's father, Darrell Madden and Brad Qualls had each made a lifelong study of the thrilling but degrading knowledge.

After Steve's nod, the car stopped a bit farther down the street, its brake lights brightening inquiringly. Darrell sauntered after it and got in on the passenger side. Steve had used his very first Social Security check to pay for this car. After a long hiatus, he was spending again. Having run through his savings, his inheritance from Aunt Marilyn, and his older brother's patience, he'd finally taken a job as a vehicle porter (and bought the "like new" Mercury) at Reynolds Ford a mere week before. He'd used his first paycheck to pay for dinner with Quentin that night.

For Darrell, once he was in the car, the tats were just a costume. He loved performance. People's attention to his lies made him feel paradoxically safe, remote, invulnerable in a suit of invisible armor. Darrell told the bald guy that he and his big friend had just come from California. As he spun the story his hands rested casually on his thighs. He was a little nervous. The bald man eyed the ripped camo. Kindly enough, he noted that it was freezing out tonight and offered to show Darrell around town. Darrell reached forward and, for luck or out of superstition, surreptitiously touched the knife through the cloth on his calf. Both he and Brad had knives on their belts, in their pockets, and strapped to their legs commando-style.

I kept trying to imagine Darrell's conversation with Steve Domer. Darrell told me about the California lie, about the cold, about Steve's offer to show him around town, about the knives. I wanted to know exactly what had been said, but naturally, no one's memory is as precise as I needed, so I made up a hypothetical exchange—hustler and john—just a few remarks, which I showed Darrell. Darrell told me the object had been to get Steve to pick up Brad as well, so I wrote his "character" asking Steve to pick up Brad because it was so cold out. After reading the exchange, the real Darrell underlined a bit of dialogue I'd given his character: "My friend is harmless, I promise." From this an arrow in black ink led to the annotation, "I also told Mr. Domer that Brad had a huge cock and loved to fuck guys. I felt I really had to do some extra convincing. Brad was really out of place."

Whatever was actually said, Steve decided to go for it.

He pulled the car around to where Brad was stationed. As Darrell keeps saying, Brad would have looked too big and straight to be a hustler-drifter from California. But the door was open now. He jumped into the backseat with a little bag which he pressed down between his feet. He mumbled a greeting but didn't even look at the bald guy. Nor did he answer when asked where he was from in California. Darrell answered for him, "He's from LA, like me." Or so I wrote in my dialogue. Darrell underlined that made-up quote too, and added, "I was so afraid that somehow my actions or mannerisms would give me away."

At a stop sign on an ill-lit street, Darrell reached over and switched the engine off. He ratcheted the gearshift to park. He did it so quickly and easily the act felt more teasing than aggressive. ("I did this very calmly so he would not get too freaked out and have everything get out of control.") Brad's arm snaked around Steve's neck from behind. Considering their positions, the one-handed pummeling that began at once may have felt inept to Steve. Brad's grunting abuse (Darrell thinks he remembers the usual "You fucking faggot") may have sounded oddly forced, like porn movie dialogue, because it was Brad's first time in this role—the whole point of this "mission" was "patching Brad out" as a foot soldier for Chaos Squad (to use their own Boy Scout–like terminology). This was the night Brad had to "show heart."[5] Darrell got out of the car and ran to the driver's side exactly the way he used to run in the opposite direction in his old limo-driving days.

According to Darrell, Brad growled, "Scoot over now!" The words stick in my mind as authentic, just because I

---

5. Benjamin Matthew Williams used similar terminology when spinning the yarn about the racist cell he'd supposedly hooked up with at Cal Expo. They demanded he "prove himself" through violent action.

would never write the absurd mommy word "scoot" in a scene like this. Steve scrambled and was dragged to the passenger-side bucket seat. Slipping into the driver's seat, Darrell kicked one of Steve's lagging feet out of the way. The engine fired with an out-of-gear screech before the car faltered up to speed.

Brad's little bag was packed with zip ties, a plastic tarp, rope, the gun, a folding shovel, changes of clothes in case they got too bloody, and two rolls of duct tape. Brad fished the metallic tape out of the bag and started binding Steve. First he pulled Steve's wrists behind his back and taped them together. With 180-foot rolls of tape, there was enough to wrap Steve almost entirely.

Steve was blindfolded next. Brad ran the tape around the man's head seven or eight times. Lengths of tape came off the roll with a furious squawking as the car lurched over potholes. When that was done, Steve's head was all but mummified. A gap was left for his nostrils and a tiny slit for his mouth, Darrell recalls.

All this time Darrell was telling Steve to follow instructions and everything would be okay. He says he ordered the bald man to bring his ankles together and lift them up. Steve did the best he could. Brad crawled forward and taped them together and elbowed Steve sharply in the balls when he was done. "I told Brad to recline Mr. Domer's seat and duct tape him to the seat [so] no one could see him from the outside." Great loops of tape started screaming off the roll again.

From that point on Steve was beaten repeatedly.

I'm not at all sure Darrell and Brad would have sounded like killers. They would have sounded more like rowdy kids. Or like braggarts—stupid, overwrought, clumsy, imprudent. Maybe (as his killers crowed later) Steve was well-behaved in spite of everything. But any survival strategies were moot: Steve had no idea what he looked like, and it was especially dangerous how little he looked like a man now, armless and bundled in metallic tape.

I asked Darrell about Steve overhearing any exchanges between him and Brad. "We had metal music playing in the car," he told me. "When we wanted to talk to each other I turned the music up even louder. The tape was over Mr. Domer's entire face as well as his ears. I'm sure he couldn't hear much anyway."

Darrell already felt he was losing control of the situation. Brad had risen to an adrenaline-fueled pitch of excitement his general had never seen before. The younger guy was quick to disagree and argue. He whaled at their prisoner and kept an eye on Darrell in the rearview mirror like a lion guarding its kill.

Darrell told Brad to look for a cell phone and wallet. Brad fished them from Steve's pockets and picked at the phone till he got the battery and SIM card out. He threw them, along with Steve's credit cards, out the window where they made a leaflike clattering on the pavement, barely audible over the radio's heavy metal. The fifty-one dollars in the wallet was such a disappointment that Brad beat Steve with extra energy to burn off the frustration.

Darrell knew the mission was getting away from him. He always counted on being the crazy one, willing to go further than anyone else. It was his special act. Without it he risked being too aware, perhaps. But Brad kept getting wilder and more self-assured. Darrell wasn't going to be able to one-up him. The thought made him uncomfortable. If the younger guy's predatory intensity wasn't exactly scaring him, it was definitely making him feel self-conscious, uncertain, maybe a little bit feminized. ("I couldn't say anything about him hitting [Mr. Domer] because of how it would have made me look.")

They kept only Steve's bank card. Darrell started interrogating Steve about his bank account and PIN number. How much money was in the account? It was a way of taking the reins from Brad. Darrell wasn't really planning on using the information. ("I knew how risky it would be to expose myself to any cameras at an ATM and gave up [asking about the PIN] after I fractured my hand on his face.") Did Steve live alone? In a whisper, the man claimed he lived with a straight older brother in Edmond, but Darrell didn't believe him. He figured Domer understood they were looking for a quiet place and didn't want them using his house. ("Our idea was we would get him somewhere we could torture him in private.") Darrell had been driving more or less blindly. He'd reached the city's far west side, the Yukon area.

"Dahmer! Fucking Dahmer!" Darrell says things got a lot worse as soon as Brad learned Steve's last name. He says Brad roared taunts like, "Dahmer is the fucking asshole who kills kids! He's your brother? This guy's related to fucking Jeffrey Dahmer. That's his faggot serial killer brother, man! You like eating boys?" With insane energy, Brad beat Steve for the similarity in names. Brad had meaty, big-boned fists that didn't injure easily. With an air of being impressed even now, Darrell says Brad "really had quite an evil streak. One that I could not control or one-up." Whether or not the following threat was actually made while they terrorized Steve, Darrell remembers it was part of the plan, something they'd chortled grimly about the previous night or on the long walk earlier: cut the faggot's dick off and stick it in his mouth or in his asshole.

Despite the knives, the shovel, the gruesome planning, Darrell also claims that at this point they were in vague accord that they were only going to beat Steve up and dump him. ("At that time [Brad] was in agreement [not to kill him]." And again, "I told Brad that he only had to rob him and beat him up . . . I told him I would still patch him out.") An hour or two had passed already. Darrell told Brad they needed to find a place in the woods somewhere and asked the other skinhead if he wanted to drive now. They switched places in Yukon.

Darrell didn't make the change because he wanted to give Steve a break. He was trying to settle Brad down for his own sake. He notes that switching places may have saved the old guy from having a rib puncture his lung or from totally racked balls—for the time being.

Volatile as Brad was, Darrell felt the need to preserve his uncertain sense of authority. He says he told Steve that they'd have to mess him up, but that they wouldn't necessarily kill him as long as he wasn't thinking about talking to the cops. Brad blew up. It was supposed to be *his* night. Pettishly he changed his mind; he decided he wanted to kill Steve after all. ("We get to talking some more and [Brad] changes his mind and now he wants to kill him, because [Mr. Domer] briefly saw what we look like." Another time, Darrell puts it, "He insisted that he kill him because he saw our faces and we would get about the same amount of time in jail if we were ever caught. He never let up about killing him.") For his own part, Darrell claims he was still thinking, or letting himself think, that the savage

talk was intended mostly to terrify Steve. ("At this time I
really think he's just saying all this to scare Mr. Domer, so
I go along.")

Brad got on I-35 heading south. He drove for half an
hour or so through the exurban sprawl of Norman, Oklahoma. As he approached the town of Goldsby, the plains
lapped at the sides of the highway. They'd left the city behind. The world became invisible beyond the dim, phos-
phorescent haze of headlights and streetlights. This was
the way home, not a good idea. But they were tired and not
thinking straight. Exit 101, right after the first Washington/
Goldsby exit, was coming up. Did Brad mean to take the
old guy to Darrell's trailer? They got off the highway and
passed the trailer several times. A third housemate was at
home.

As Brad drove, Darrell searched the car. He pulled the
backseat cushion forward and reached into the trunk,
polymer-scented, well-carpeted. It was empty except for a
few dry-cleaners' coat hangers.

The two skinheads argued off and on. The boastful,
huffy way Brad insisted on killing Steve made Darrell
doubt him still. It sounded too much like a child's exhausted petulance. Nevertheless, they stopped on a country road and switched places again. Darrell headed east on
Ladd Road, still too close to Washington and the trailer,
but they'd been driving for four hours. Drained, Darrell
found it hard to argue, even to speak. Ladd Road made a
big dip. Two large gas wells on the right-hand side nodded tediously the way they do all over Oklahoma. Then the
road flattened out between fields. Somewhere along here,
Steve was killed.

Darrell describes the sequence of events: "We ask him

if he wants to suck our dongs before we kill him. He says
yes that he did. I think he thought we were kidding too.
We got near my house and Brad asks me how he should
kill him and I tell him about the hangers in the backseat. I
told him to untwist the hanger to make it a straight piece
of metal wire and put it around his neck with his foot on
his back, pull real hard, and twist it like a bread tie. I'm
saying this real loud to scare Mr. Domer."

Brad pulled the rear seat cushion forward and reached
for one of the coat hangers. He shook it loose, ripped the
paper and plastic off, and laboriously unwound it. From
behind, Brad slipped the hanger wire around Steve's neck
and pulled it tight. Steve's taped head nodded upward
over Brad's fists. The wire disappeared into laps of skin
and a loop of Steve's gold chain slipped from a gap in the
tape. Darrell glanced from the road to the mummy beside
him. The chain glimmered, sidling across the silver tape.
After a moment or two, Brad kicked his foot up onto the
car seat and planted it against the back of Steve's neck. He
pulled harder. He flapped one hand loosely in the air and
regripped the wire.

It became clear to Darrell that Brad wasn't just terrifying the old man. This was a killing. He says he felt badly
about it in a far-off way, but that he immediately started
worrying about dumping the body. He fancied himself an
orderly criminal. Practicalities took over. A deeper, chaotic
part of him understood they wouldn't get away with this.
That fate hung in the air from the beginning. (Darrell mentions an early "realization that I was going to get caught."
He adds, "To be completely honest with you, I had no feelings whatsoever after the fact. Only that I let this dumb-ass
take control from me . . . I was surely going to get caught. It

was only a matter of time. I did want to get caught eventually, but I had a lot of things I wanted to do before I did.")

Up ahead, a flat concrete bridge ran over the gully on the left side of the road. Built for farm machinery, it led to a fence and a vast plowed field abutting Hat Ranch beyond. Without thinking Darrell turned, and the car bucked onto the bridge over streaks of red earth. The gully, with a dribble of a creek in it, ran in front of a hedgerow of scrub, twisted old cottonwood trees and Osage oranges, already dropping flaming rust leaves. The glimpse of color—red earth, rust leaves—vanished when Darrell killed the headlights. They tipped the body over the low railing of the bridge. Darrell explains: "I get out of the car and pick up Mr. Domer. I bump his head on the concrete wall. Brad winces. I throw him over and we hear a little splash as his feet hit the edge of the water." The body landed on a patch of earth near the opening of the bridge culvert. To Darrell the mission felt messy.

They returned to I-35 and drove on. Southbound still, with Brad at the wheel. They got a second wind. Now Brad became giddy. He seemed to find himself too powerful just to sit there in the car. He continually shifted and bounced in his seat and howled and bragged that this wasn't his first. He said he'd killed Jimmy Fite in Ardmore, though Darrell didn't believe him. (Chasse Stevens would later go to prison for that murder.[6])

Darrell tried to relax. He tried to relish the mission. But Brad's domineering excitement irritated him. He kept

---

6. The Ardmore Sheriff Department's chief investigator in the case, Rick Batt, says Qualls wasn't involved and knew neither Fite nor Stevens. A juvenile whom Brad did know boasted about taking a video of Fite's body and may have helped dump it in a stream. Supposedly, Brad destroyed the video to protect the juvenile whom he called "a dumb kid." That was how Brad found out about this little-publicized murder and ended up being questioned about it.

hearing himself make out that he was an old hand at all of this. For some reason the control problem ruined it for him.

Brad took I-35 all the way down to Ardmore—an hour, two hours. They stopped at a gas station, spent some of Steve's money on a can of gas and Copenhagen, and switched drivers again. They went to the house of another Chaos Squad friend. At three or four a.m. Darrell and Brad roused him. He was wearing dingy underwear, and, when he turned, inviting them in, a swastika glistened on his shoulder as if wet. He refused their proposal outright. He was terrified but tried to hide the fact with a pantomime of grogginess. Darrell's idea was to take him to see the body. Then, the very next night, he and the guy would go out and kill another one.

The point was that Brad hadn't been a good match. He was too straight, too big, oafish, unattractive, too over-whelming when he started going wild. Darrell needed to replay the whole episode. Something he couldn't identify had been missing. Perhaps the missing element was desire, even love. And this guy, this Ardmore brother, was one he loved, a proper skinhead. (Darrell tells me now, "This guy was real cute. I did lots of tattoos on him. Every time I got hard. He always liked showing off his dick too. I really liked this guy.")

Since it felt like their lives were now hurtling toward an end, Brad and Darrell wanted to start killing again soon. The Chaos Squad brother's refusal was infuriat-ing. The conversation was tense, inarticulate, unfriendly. Chaos Squad rules were being flouted, but no one had the alertness to figure out what needed to be done about it. The prim confusion when Darrell and Brad left—tattooed thugs acting like disappointed parents—made it clear a threat would be coming later. Brad talked about killing the Ardmore brother almost immediately.

This visit was strange. Darrell explains, "We wanted to make the other member a part of it. Kind of like a three-pact deal even though it was against the rules. The rules say if you are not part of the deal you don't get details and you don't need to know. Afterward, Brad wants to kill more, anyone. Especially the member who did not do as asked."

The rest of that predawn passed in an exhausted back-and-forth. Darrell and Brad bickered. They needed to get rid of the car. But Brad was tired and stubborn. In Ardmore he'd stopped in briefly at another friend's house and cadged a joint. Darrell says that after smoking the joint Brad became paranoid.

I've pressed Darrell many times about what happened next, a visit to a porn store. Frankly, I wanted to know whether the murder was arousing. Or did Brad, after a night of hypermasculinity and violence, simply want *some* form of feminine solace, even if it was pornographic and on glossy paper? Darrell says he doesn't know. ("I'm not sure what was on Brad's mind when we went to the porn store. All I know is that he really wanted to go. Of course, what was on my mind was what if we see me on a box cover or poster in the store? Yikes! Of course, I do look a little different, but in my mind . . .") They got back on I-35 and continued south about forty minutes beyond Ardmore.

Oklahoma bans hard-core pornography, so they had to go to the porn store conveniently located just across the Texas state line, exactly the way a big casino, banned in Texas, is located on this side of the border. Once over the nondescript Red River bridge separating the two states, Brad and Darrell would have seen the big sign for DW's Adult Video on the right even before they noticed the little one: *Welcome to Texas, Proud Home of President George W. Bush.* When Darrell got out of the car, the glue of duct tape plucked at his T-shirt.

The thing Darrell was worried about—surges of sleep-deprived and irrational alarm—was that they'd walk in and see a big poster for *By Private Invitation of Billy Houston* or pass the tiny male section in the far corner of the barnlike space and see the cover of *Headbangers*. He knew of a skinhead who'd done a jack-off video; it didn't go well for him when his brothers found out. To the right as you entered DW's was a wall of dildos and sex toys, then endless Walmart-like aisles of DVDs. They wandered. They looked. ("There was no peepshow. We didn't buy any magazines.") There was no point to it.

Darrell's eyes hurt after a few minutes under glaring fluorescent light. Coming out of DW's, the darkness was welcome. He rubbed his eyes with his good hand. The edges of his field of vision warped and glimmered as if someone were dangling Steve's gold chain just out of sight.

Brad had patched out from "prospect" to "foot sol-dier." But the mission wasn't over yet. Originally Darrell meant to take the car back to Oklahoma City and ditch it there. They'd have to walk the eighteen miles to Washing-ton again. Brad complained that his feet were hurting. He was too tired. Darrell suggested they swing by the trailer in Washington where he had two dirt bikes. They could load them in the trunk and ride home after dumping the car. But Brad was too tired even for that. Darrell didn't have the energy to insist. He'd begun to nurse a sense of fatality. He knew how to get rid of evidence so it stays gone—he says he's had plenty of experience—but it seemed to matter less this time. The end of everything was within sight.

During the early stages of the beating, Darrell had refractured an old boxer's break in his hand. It was starting to swell, and holding the steering wheel hurt. He continued to let Brad drive. Despite the excuse of the injured hand, his own passivity felt unforgivable.

Lengths of tape still stuck to the passenger seat. (Darrell adds, "There was also some blood on the seat from Mr. Domer's nose and face. I put one of the floor mats over it in order to sit down without getting blood on my BDUs [Battle Dress Uniforms].") But the murder already seemed unreal. Maybe for that reason, Brad and Darrell drove back up to Ladd Road to look at the body as if they were showing it to their Ardmore brother, after all. ("Still there. What did we think, it was going to get up and walk away?") The body was near the culvert. The feet just touched the water in the creek. A gigantic pupa in dully gleaming tape. A dapper bend at the waist was the most human thing about it.

Using the can of gasoline they'd bought with Steve Domer's fifty-one dollars, they torched the car at SE 12th Avenue and Cottonwood Road, a bare five- or ten-minute walk from home. The burned car would be found right away. After the body was discovered more than a week after that, police started canvassing the area. When asked if anybody gay lived thereabouts, neighbors recalled that Darrell Madden had been living with another man in his trailer—and had even been arrested for domestic abuse one time. It must have been obvious where to look, though. In an area of tidy, expensive-looking horse farms, the single yellowish, run-down, white-trash trailer with its kennel of

German shepherds sticks out like a sore thumb. By that time Brad was dead and Darrell was lashed to a hospital bed in Oklahoma City.

For now the two skinheads talked about murder, the next murder. Footsore, they walked from the burning car. The car alarm started screaming. They hurried. Brad had quieted now. Darrell held his swollen hand at chest level to keep it from throbbing. They decided they were going to have to kill that Ardmore Chaos brother who'd refused them. He knew too much; he hadn't come through. For Darrell, self-immolating desire also cast its glow on this fantasy or plan. Of all of them, that perfect skinhead brother aroused him most. Climbing the grayed and warped board steps to the trailer, Darrell and Brad were already going over details of the planned murder.

Darrell later summarizes: "Brad argues about walking back, biking back, or anything else. Too tired. I guess I was too. I felt I had lost control. Gave in and set the car on fire without disconnecting the battery about one mile from home. Very loud alarm. Oops! Get home. Look out back bedroom at fire. It's a wonder you could not hear the alarm or see the lights flashing pointed right at the trailer. [The other housemate] wakes up. Was sleeping in my bedroom. Brad says, 'Let's kill him too.'" Though he was tired beyond conceiving, Darrell had to take three Seroquel to fall asleep.

Seroquel is an antipsychotic used off-label for sleep and often abused (especially in California prisons) because it isn't a controlled substance. Darrell got his first prescription for it in prison.

Darrell awoke in a fog. At some point during the day,

the third housemate (he'd just been asked to move out despite the fact that he and Darrell were close—they knew each other's secrets) overheard Darrell and Brad talking about a man who wouldn't fight back. Though the housemate didn't realize he was ever a target himself, he later went to the police.

When Darrell and Brad checked up on the Ardmore brother they planned to kill, they learned he'd left town hours after seeing them. He'd gone to take a job on an oil rig. They tried his cell phone. He spoke to them briefly but refused to say where he was.

The night after the murder, Darrell and Brad invited some people over to the trailer. This was when Brad told his mother, Tina Melton, that he'd killed someone, the confession Darrell made him take back by e-mail. Perhaps it was now, not earlier, when the housemate overheard them going on about the man who didn't fight back. Even discounting the specter of recent murder, it wasn't much of a party: TV on in the background (no reports about a missing Steve Domer yet, but soon), Jack Daniel's, beer, Coke, chips, smokes. Darrell tells me, "During this party my girlfriend made 'the eye' at me, so I took her, and my gun, in my room and fucked her. I faked getting off once she came." Brad got a little drunk. He fought with his own girlfriend. At one point—it must have been later—he took the gun out of the black bag and left the trailer. Darrell soon discovered him alone outside. When Brad threatened to kill himself, Darrell says he had to wrestle the gun from him. He remembers being surprised that his hulking co-murderer couldn't put up more of a fight. Darrell says he fired once at the ground at Brad's feet and said, "I'll help you [kill yourself]." As he did twenty nights later.

After the tussle, Darrell's body throbbed, the insects chirred, Brad panted. Life seemed about to dissolve. In his heart Darrell blamed Brad for everything sloppy about the mission, for everything that had turned bad.

They visited the body at least four times over the next week. In daylight the skin of the bald head was visible, waxen blue-gray, unreal-looking, flecked with dirt. They wondered if it had been moved slightly by an animal. They kept going back.

III. *Oklahoma*

When I walked into the Oklahoma City motel's ordinary glass vestibule I found a four-foot-tall model of the World Trade Center complete with *Never Forget* regalia. I happened to have been living a couple of blocks from the World Trade Center when it was destroyed. My experience that day was personal and local. But I'd long ago gotten used to ceding "my" disaster to the rest of the country as a political whatnot, so I just snorted to myself and checked in, and it took me several days before I realized the big model wasn't the usual display of patriotic schmaltz. It was also personal and local. Oklahoma City and New York are dissimilar in every way except that both have been the victims of terror. A quick trip to the Murrah memorial in downtown Oklahoma City makes the close parallel between the cities' experiences obvious. The sense of cousinship is more deeply felt here in Oklahoma. New Yorkers are too ready to be disliked and too wrapped up in themselves to notice a little friendly feeling way out here.

Though friendliness is a point of pride here, I sense underneath it a stubborn mistrust. Maybe it's a distant Dust Bowl memory, but the state's personality, despite the oil boom that ended around 1981, is still basically rural and poor, self-consciously backward, suspicious. The *Daily Oklahoman* is wearily mocked as the *Daily Disappointment*. Religion feels urgent here, a land of inarticulate big-sky angst, yet it can also become the tool of a small-town mean-spiritedness which is older than Christianity, older than religion itself. This is death penalty country. If Darrell Madden's background hadn't been outstandingly awful, the goal of prosecutors would have been execution.

When I visit Mort Domer, Steve's brother, at the Edmond house he and Steve used to share, where he now lives with a woman he's married since the trial, he announces how he warned family members that he planned to tell it to me like it was. He does. We sit at a kitchen counter drinking iced tea. Mort's wife sits a little distance away in the adjoining living room, politely only half-participating in the conversation. Mort is tired, not from the cancer he recently beat back but from the effort to understand his brother and what happened to him. He asks for Darrell's address, because he's considering a ministry about forgiveness for his church.

From where we sit, the Domers can illustrate the story by pointing. Down the hall was Steve's room packed high with ornaments, T-shirts, junk. Right here off the living room is the sunroom Steve built onto the modest house. Its high ceiling and tile floor and expensive windows illustrate Steve's slightly grand tastes. Here under the sink is where they found bottles and bottles of wine. Not Steve's—he wasn't a big drinker—they must have belonged to one of the boyfriends. Mort says this with characteristic gravelly wryness. The boyfriends didn't like Mort much. Mort saw what was going on with them.

There are many crosses on the walls now, and family photographs. Everyday talk of Jesus is close to the surface, restrained a bit out of politeness or uncertainty about me. None of us insists too much on the looming "gay" issue. Clearly it's a religious conundrum for them. The notion is mentioned in passing—full of discomfort, but as something hard *not* to think—that Steve's lifestyle and end were somehow, on some level, connected.

For lunch we go to an ex–Long John Silver's tricked out as a Mexican restaurant with a ceramic Aztec calendar, a donkey planter, and the odd sombrero on the walls. We join hands and pray. Mort's wife mentions how the murder flickers on in their lives in the most preposterous ways. Just yesterday they finally received a check from the state reimbursing them thirty-eight dollars for Steve's toll pass, which burned in his car. She shakes her head at the strangeness of it.

Initially, they did talk of the death penalty for Steve Domer's murder. Mort spoke to the Oklahoma County DA, David Prater, who told him a death penalty conviction would be tricky given Darrell's background. In any case, Mort, an eye on his own mortality, wanted the case resolved. With Prater acting as go-between, Darrell agreed to plead guilty in return for life without parole.

Before the plea, Mort and Darrell sat alone together at a table in the courtroom and talked about what happened for thirty minutes. Mort first gave Darrell a Bible, then asked him, "If you were the leader of this thing, how could you let it happen the way it did?" And Darrell talked honestly about the murder, spoke a little of his past, admitted he was gay, and cried. Afterward, the judge himself came down from the bench to hug Mort.

Television reports claimed Mort asked for the meeting, yet Mort to this day believes it was Darrell's idea. It was arranged by DA Prater, who impressed on Darrell that had his own brother been murdered he'd want to know what happened.

On reflection Mort himself doesn't know whether Darrell's tears came more from relief or remorse, but his forgiveness stands. At the time he felt the tears were real. He describes how Darrell had transformed before his eyes from the smirking and remote figure of the trial's first days into the vulnerable, badly damaged man who sat across that table talking to him.

I have a hard time locating the exact place Darrell and Brad dumped Steve's body. I drive back and forth past Darrell's old yellow trailer (leaving a long note for the occupant, who never contacts me). I'm looking for a little bridge but there are a number of them around. Following the road in one direction I pass a tiny grass airstrip and soon get turned around among eroded dirt roads that peter out in a gas field near the Goldsby water tower. Somebody would have mentioned the water tower. I go the other way. Once I think I've found the place, but the bridge is too close to Hat Ranch. All the while I'm taking notes with my right hand, driving with my left: *gravel—cow grate after airfield—sort of paved—horses everywhere—equine hospital—gully and tree row—cottonwood—red, red earth.* The car is a mess of papers, maps, pens, soda cans, and empty potato chip bags.

Eventually, I find the bridge. Not what I expected, but it fits. The car bounces up onto the concrete bed of the span and I park. I take a lot of pictures; I'm insatiable for detail. The nagging question of whether I'm more Steve or more

Darrell evaporates in a sunny sense of discovery and satisfaction. The murder has become everyday work for me. Like the famously "heartless" artist, I'm frankly pleased to recall how Darrell described the body's head hitting this very railing and Brad's, the killer's, sympathetic wince for a corpse. It's a strange and telling detail. Once more, self-conscious worry chills my skin and vanishes.

The wonder is how such a violent, charming, false character as Darrell's is formed. Can it be beaten into any kid? What about Brad? At the same time, the early '90s, that Darrell was getting into porn in LA, Bradley Qualls was still a boy in Ardmore. Virtually friendless, he was often beaten up. His sister Michelle had to fight on his behalf sometimes. Brad was irritating, overactive, and just couldn't learn. He was tormented for this by other kids. Of course, he was diagnosed with ADHD and served up a slew of medications.

Michelle puts the most dramatic change in Brad's personality at around fourteen. He resolved to fight back. It's when he decided to go off medication, but it's also the moment when adolescent hormones really do change the brain. Depression and mental illness often first show up around that age. Brad was big, he'd learned how to fight through being beaten, and now he started running wild. He started protecting his sister instead of the other way around. Michelle says he was always ripe to join, to be a part of something. After being released from prison that first time, he was proud of getting a driver's license, a car, a girlfriend, proud of getting off drugs with the encouragement of Chaos Squad. Michelle still remembers how excited he was the day he told her he was finally going to get to meet the leader.

Darrell's background was different. You want to believe there is and always was something wrong with him,
something psychopathic. Things start to fall into place
when you learn his uncle and father both suffered serious
mental illness. His father, diagnosed a paranoid schizo-
phrenic, was in and out of mental hospitals. And yet . . .
the man wasn't Darrell's real father. Darrell doesn't know
who his real father was. The simple genetic theory has to
be scratched.

As a kid Darrell was brutalized like Brad, but for a different reason. In Darrell's case he was treated with contempt as a faggot. School got so insufferable for the pretty,
vaguely effeminate boy that he habitually skipped out.
A school bus driver who Darrell now believes had a bit
of a crush on him connived in his absences, suggesting,
"Here might be a good spot to slip off the bus, boy." Darrell
would run back home and hide in a chicken coop where
he'd spend the day listening to the radio and reading magazines. He couldn't let his mom find out. He doted on her,
and between her work as a butcher at IGA and a husband
too ill to work himself, she had a wearying life. She didn't
need more worries.

After his uncle was divorced, Darrell and his father
used to stop by his house to check on him. The man took
the breakup badly, and sure enough, one day they walked
in and found him dead, blood everywhere. Darrell's father made him and his sister clean up the mess, and Darrell still remembers vividly the thick, jellied quality of the
half-set blood. He was about fourteen. A year and a half
later, sneaking into his henhouse refuge, Darrell came upon
his father hanging from a beam, blue. Though he says he
doesn't remember it, he cut his father down and saved his

life. Only briefly. His father died soon afterward. A new stepfather brought the school violence and dislike home to Darrell.

By this time Darrell had learned that his appearance brought unlooked-for power with a certain type of man—for example, the "real estate agent" who showed him around an empty house and casually turned and dropped his pants.

Darrell probably went to the gay neighborhood in Oklahoma City a few times even at this age. Some people there remember him as a kid. But soon he left town for Houston with an African American drag queen and a few other friends. In Houston he saw his first skinhead and fell in love—not with the person but with the type, the idea. His friends warned him he couldn't have anything to do with guys like that, because they'd just as soon kill him. Darrell took that as a challenge.

There are skinheads all over the country and the world. Neo-Nazi groups in Eastern Europe, Pinoy gangs in LA and Manila, the LA Death Squad (LADS). Often they're surprisingly casual about the Aryan issue. There's even one nonracist group, SHARP, Skinheads Against Racial Prejudice. It's a young man's game. It isn't unusual to start at thirteen. The majority are seventeen- and eighteen-year-olds. Still in it at thirty-seven at the time of the murders, Darrell was an anomaly.

Like most gangs, skinhead culture thrives on naïve passions and loyalties. A streak of nerdiness is reflected in endless rules and ranks and taboos and secret emblems. The solidarity the group engenders is, basically, love. Thinking about this solidarity can make an intellectual, a grown-up, even a gay person or a Jew, feel, besides scorn or anger, a slight, inarticulate embarrassment, a superannuated yearning for the simple emotion of youth. This is the dangerous, illusory moral *feeling* that Fascism has always played to.

Unlike overtly political or religious organizations of the kind that fascinated Ben Williams—the Aryan Nations, Christian Identity, etc.—skinheads often don't have much of a program. They're kids, strays, squatters, runaways, members of the angry white underclass, disposable boys who band together out of fury and for protection. Their rebellious anger is often mistaken for real rebellion. More commonly, the shock of growing up, of glimpsing all the different and conflicting mores out there in the world, prompts a kind of nauseated conservatism. Whether they mean to or not, they become the crazed enforcers of the values of their fathers and mothers.

But for Darrell, more clearly than for most, the skinheads meant love. An alloy emotion "love-fear" describes it better, because for Darrell the love was steeped in deceit, mistrust, lies, the possibility of treachery. He was forever on the alert. He had to will himself to appear as steady as the dealer's hand the moment before the fatal card is turned over.

The skinhead's tribal racism and anti-Semitism and loathing for homosexuals was easy enough to pick up. Darrell's parents had been prosaic, unimpassioned racists. Blacks were "niggers." OKC was "Niggertown." It wasn't harmless, but it wasn't intensely felt either—more backward-looking, unimaginative, and lazy. It was easy for Darrell to dial up the hatred so that the brotherly love would become, by contrast, even sweeter.

For example, a perfect sublimation of this love might

have come at one of those Chaos Squad tattoo parties less than a year before the murders. Darrell was with the Ardmore Chaos brother who later refused to join him and Brad on their spree. Darrell talks about this person repeatedly with desire in his voice. "He was little, perfect body, always running around showing off his little dick." Perhaps it was outside, a summer afternoon. A "skinbyrd" girlfriend watched, yawned, batted a bee away. The boys straddled a bench. Slouching as far as his spine permitted, the brother offered his pallid back to Darrell, who meticulously pricked a swastika into the skin over the guy's shoulder blade with the whining ink gun. Darrell would have felt his brother's wincing as he steadied his fingers and forearm on the infinitely soft skin. As he says, he'd always get hard.

Oklahoma seems tough on its children, like a badly educated parent. Time and again before interviews, I found myself holding hands around the table in prayer. Our bowed heads, our extravagant humility, felt propitiatory. Then the interviews would turn to the kind of seedy, raucous lives glimpsed on certain TV shows, where the country's underclass likes to make a spectacle of itself as we watch and call it pop culture. Here, since the point wasn't ratings or harsh amusement, the stories were suffused with sadness and incomprehension.

After I visited a women's shelter in Ardmore, word got around that I was looking into Bradley Qualls's background. Rumors swirled about the Fite case, the other murder Brad had been questioned about before he was killed. When I got back to New York I received a pleading call from Chasse Stevens's mother. Her son had gone to prison swearing he didn't kill Fite. Was there anything I could do?

"Sir, you have to understand, this is a very corrupt place."
I couldn't say the case was only a small detail, a footnote
in my story, because it was her son's life. She had such a
misplaced notion of my power as a writer. The grimness of
the Osage Plains seemed to blow through the phone.

During his time away in Southern California, Darrell may
have acquired a little Los Angeles glamour with which to
impress the locals when he returned to spend the seven
years before Steve Domer's murder back in Oklahoma. This
part of his story reads almost like an outlaw saga, something
I don't like. He was in misery and spreading it. It's difficult
to convey the sometimes desperate energy of self-repression.
"Gay" was such a monkey on his back that Darrell was in
constant existential contortion. The contrast between California and Oklahoma may only have heightened things.

In 1999, Darrell was paroled from a California prison.
He'd been in on a narcotics charge. The highlife in LA had
spiraled to its inevitable end. In a common arrangement
called an "interstate compact," California handed him off
to the Oklahoma Department of Corrections, which super-
vised his parole. He was monitored by an officer in the town
of Purcell, Oklahoma. Darrell went to live with his mother
in McClain County (a couple of years later she moved
out and left the rickety yellow trailer to him). Through a
brother-in-law he got a job operating heavy equipment at
Huddleston Construction in Oklahoma City. The worka-
day world wasn't easy for someone used to the life he'd
lived. After about ten months, he got into a bad fight with
his brother-in-law and quit Huddleston. He worked as a
motel clerk for a year.

When money was tight he'd slip into Oklahoma City to

spend a weekend night dancing naked at Tramps. He stood on a big black plywood box right by the entrance. (I tell him the box is still there, though they don't have dancers anymore.) Even here, even dancing, even around people who knew him, he could still sometimes play "not gay" to himself. Buoyed by a cloud of contempt, he danced like he wasn't feeling anything—like he was actually untouchable—even when some idiot was reaching into his underwear to wrap a dollar bill around his cock. Occasionally he trolled for clients at the An-Son car wash across the street. That was why he later feared recognition at the spot.

But he was getting long in the tooth for that kind of work and wanted to leave it behind. He got his real estate license and started selling for Coldwell Banker in northwest Oklahoma City. He did pretty well.

Then he met a boy. This was always much harder to accept than dancing or hustling. Darrell wanted to be straight more than anything. The masculinity that obsessed him was the adolescent kind defined as much by a studied repulsion for the boys you're at ease with as it is by desire for the girls who make you uncomfortable. At the same time he was, almost reflexively, an expert seducer. He might have looked a touch dumb with his close-set eyes, but when he got talking, you realized how smart he was. He had a gentle, insinuating voice without a trace of a yokel Sooner accent. When he and the new kid started talking the language of dating and love, however, Darrell's articulateness abandoned him. His head ached as if he had an allergy to awareness of this kind of thing—love between men. He'd go silent and brood. The wrongness of it was more than he could take. His own ingrained opinions seemed to echo from the minds of people on the streets or in stores. It wasn't him thinking—it was the entire world. In his body he felt a constant, deep, maddening buzz of moral disgust and dishonor.

The boy he dated, from a broken home in Norman, was his usual: slim, hairless, a lot younger—nineteen when they met. He wasn't particularly beautiful, which made Darrell feel more in control. In fact, the kid's homeliness was arousing. Darrell held all the cards. But the boy swished and minced and bitched and whined and lisped! Darrell couldn't order the sissified airs out of his lover. In public, he fumed. Everyone assumed they were gay, of course. It was grotesque. Darrell knew he wasn't the most masculine-seeming guy in the world himself.

On top of the gayness, the kid had had way too much sexual experience. He admitted bottoming several times for a thirteen-year-old Norman neighbor. As a sometime hustler, Darrell had never come at a relationship from the patriarchal, possessive side. It felt a little ludicrous. He started getting jealous. Apparently he didn't hold all the cards. His feelings became intense, obsessive.

Their set-to of desire and rancor passed for love. When the boy couldn't stay off AOL chat, Darrell started worrying he was setting up dates, or as he says brutally now, "plotting to get more dick up his ass." They fought, they broke up, they tried to get back together. The love, or whatever it was, turned into unrelieved pain. Revenge fantasies turned into tawdry revenge. The boy called the Real Estate Commission and told them Darrell had lied about his prison background when applying for his license. The license was revoked. Darrell told the cops about that thirteen-year-old neighbor, and his ex-lover was convicted of lewd molestation. Even now, from prison, Darrell crows, "I won!"

For Darrell, the experience proved yet again that "gay" was just morbid impermanence. It couldn't be his life. He was already working part time for 5 Star Limousine of Oklahoma City. With no more real estate money coming in, he started working full time driving party limos and six-door Cadillac Fleetwood funeral cars. His easy friendliness with strangers served him well. But the breakup was surprisingly hard to get over. He started shooting up cocaine—cocaine because the meth in Oklahoma just wasn't as good as he'd been used to in California. He'd binge for a few days, then stay off it for a while. Even so, things started going downhill the way they do with drugs.

During this time, Darrell may have been working with the police as a confidential informant in narcotics investigations. After the murders, an anonymous poster on a local website claimed that Darrell used to set up acquaintances for busts. The anonymous poster's gossip is incredibly important—it might say volumes about Darrell's double nature—but I haven't verified it. If the confidential informant story is true, it could help explain the odd transformation Darrell went through next.

When "gay" didn't work out, Darrell gave up on that and started impersonating a cop. He lied about his criminal background to the Oklahoma Council on Law Enforcement Education and Training (CLEET) and took a job as a security guard. (In the four months he was employed, he was promoted to "lieutenant.") Given the new job, no one asked questions when he started outfitting himself with police paraphernalia. Cuffs, a vest, a holster. He got a T-shirt emblazoned with *OCPD*. He bought a used 1998 Crown Victoria, an ex–police cruiser, freshened the paint, added new strobes and a siren. He was set.

He started prowling the Will Rogers Courts area of Oklahoma City, a mostly poor African American part of town. He felt the racist imperative to prey on a tribe apart, and he may have thought rightly that poor African Americans were more likely to be cowed by or not question a corrupt cop. Like the gay crowds he'd danced for at Tramps, an audience he found contemptible would concentrate his performance. The scheme went amazingly well. He "confiscated" drugs, cash, and guns, and the men he pulled over—only African American men, he specifies—were all but grateful to get off scot-free.

I find these performances almost as hard to imagine as I do Darrell's rages or his tearful outbursts. He must have performed with insane concentration to make the impersonation plausible. But you get the sense around this time that his life and "acts" are already getting out of hand.

Darrell was having a feud with a neighbor in Washington. The man ran one of the small llama farms which had become faddish during the past decade. One of Darrell's German shepherds, wolfishly frisky at four months, kept escaping her pen and running the animals down. Threats had been exchanged. Darrell returned to the trailer one day and found his dog shot dead. Though sheep, and presumably llama, farmers have a widely recognized right to shoot dogs that harass their livestock, Darrell thought his neighbor killed his "puppy" because he was personally frightened. Darrell became enraged and called the police, the real police. No one called back. No one came to the trailer. No one seemed to know about the complaint when Darrell followed up days later.

The next time Darrell was out by Will Rogers Courts, he pulled over a young black man who turned out to be an off-duty cop. It was a quick exchange. Darrell jumped away from the driver's-side window and ran for his car. He left the strobes on, and they throbbed red, white, and blue as he sped off. The off-duty cop clapped his own siren and LED to his dashboard and set off after the police cruiser. Because he had no radio to call for backup, Darrell got away.

But now the trailer in Washington didn't feel safe. A day or two later, overcome by rage and stress, Darrell marched out and shot seven of his neighbor's llamas. Six died. If he did have secret police contacts, they may have recognized his name when officers looked into the llama case. Darrell now says only that he was reached a month or two after the car chase and told to present himself at police headquarters along with his Crown Victoria and that he told them, "Go fuck yourself and try and come get me." They got him. He was arraigned. Animal cruelty and impersonating a police officer. He posted bail.

Darrell decided to run. On eBay he sold the Crown Victoria to a man in Oregon. He had to wait a few weeks for the $4,100 money order to arrive. He never sent the title. Darrell looked up a hustler friend from the An-Son car wash, another hairless, slim youngster. He'd always had a thing for this kid. He held out the thrill of being on the run, his ten thousand or so dollars in cash, all told, and his very real passion, and the kid bit.

The two boys drove to Mexico in the Crown Victoria. The story rated a couple of mentions in the *Oklahoman*. "Purcell Police are searching for a Washington man wanted in connection with an Internet scam." "A Washington man wanted on several warrants may have fled the country, investigators say."

144 🌱 American Honor Killings

Darrell and the kid made it all the way to Acapulco and drifted into a private end-times of sex and dope. They lost weight. In Mexico Darrell dropped to a spooky 130 pounds or so. They lost their passports. From twilight to twilight the same Baudelairean day kept repeating itself. It was the kind of life that's debilitating to live but eerily lovely to remember. And Darrell does now remember the episode as the sexually ecstatic center of his life. Passports gone, the boys made love and sniggered at how they were white wetbacks. The joke suited Darrell; he was born the reverse of everything.

The interlude didn't last long. After a telephone tip from back home, Mexican police picked the lovers up and sent them to a hellish facility in Mexico City where they languished until a flight to Houston was arranged. The hustler-boyfriend was greeted by his agonized mother. The police greeted Darrell.

Even before his plea deal, Darrell realized that, once again, "gay" had to evaporate like a dream. He spent the next fifteen months in the Jess Dunn Correctional Center. Predictably, he gravitated to the skinheads. Attraction and identification were more or less the same thing. He had to prove himself, method act, insinuate himself among guys he believed hated him. Here, apparently, he found Chaos Squad.

Darrell's specialty, perfected in California, was to play the Tasmanian devil, the little guy who makes up for what he lacks in stature with sheer craziness. He could never be the lumbering giant whose prison poker face and ropey muscles projected unassailable masculinity without effort. Instead, Darrell kept fellow prisoners awed and off-balance with his violence and ruthlessness. Words alone, joking about some insane cruelty, were often enough to startle much bigger, quieter men.

The constant irony was that daily life among the skinheads in prison was strikingly similar to scenes from the gay porn movies Darrell had appeared in not long before in California. He was aware of it even at the time, though he could twist himself into half-believing in his straightness. Sometimes a group of guys would all raucously pull out their dicks for comparison. The rough camaraderie sounds pretty gay but wasn't. Darrell suppressed any desires with a healthy fear of death. Likewise, prison banter was both true and untrue. Buddies threatened, "Better not be looking at my dick." Now Darrell admits, "Of course, I always did look." You could beat off with your buddy, but if you were somehow "gay," the same buddy might beat the life out of you. The difference amounted to the thickness of a playing card, facedown.

This experience hammered into Darrell something he'd always known: "gay" was a global form of betrayal. It's why in California he could hustle and gay-bash in the same day, perhaps why he could set up busts as a confidential informant for the police, why he was able to kill Brad, his own pledge and partner, why he now must fear for his life as a Chaos Squad "traitor," and why he says his greatest worry is how gays "will treat me when they find out I have killed some of my own people. Yes, I said *some*."

IV. Los Angeles and Truth

I sent Darrell an old photograph of himself and he tells me he remembers the occasion well. Billy Houston, as he was known, had taken off his clothes. Behind him a few shaggy trees filtered golden light. He and the photographer and a guy holding a bendable circular diffuser were in Griffith Park in Los Angeles. It was a photo shoot for a small gay magazine called *In Touch*. But the pictures would eventually be used as stills for one of Billy's first XXX performances for the director Richard Lawrence. (The original Richard Lawrence. Something of a humorist among porn directors, his name was later appropriated by a more prolific, unfunny director.) This was 1991. Darrell had just turned twenty-one.

As Billy, Darrell had just one tattoo: *Jamie* in italics on his left shoulder. (Darrell explains, "He was the love of my life for a while. He was a very young dancer I met at a coffee shop in West Hollywood . . . He was really OPENLY gay . . . He would try to hold hands and I would push him away forcibly.") For the photograph Darrell wore underwear and a blue jean jacket. The cuffs of the jacket were rolled back two turns. He hooked his thumbs in the waistband of his Calvin Kleins and tugged down a few inches. At a distance two passersby—some gay hookup probably, Darrell says—slowed down to watch and grinned. Looking right through them, Billy smiled. Unlike many porn actors, he had a dazzling smile.

His light brown hair fell in a silky mop over his forehead and the tops of his ears. Hanging open, the jean jacket showed that otherwise he didn't have a hair on him. His eyes, which appeared cutely crossed, were a little close-set for perfect beauty. They squinted and drooped when the dimpled smile crept across his face like syrup. He looked like a young Jan-Michael Vincent. He had the same endearing dopiness. But unlike the old Disney star, Billy's appeal was highlighted by a touch of harmless wickedness.

* * *

Though they're hard to find, I tracked down and watched some of Darrell's pornographic movies and was baffled and disturbed. He's very young-looking and has a distinct hint of "gay" in his voice. His acting is a little more developed than the average, his sex a lot less so. He stars in an early one, *The Devil and Danny Webster*, without doing much. He plays an unpopular, supposedly unattractive, glasses-wearing geek who makes a trial pact with the devil to become the most popular guy in West Hollywood. As the film opens, the character walks by the very shopping plaza Darrell later tells me was his favorite hustling spot. For the big "transformation" from geek to god, he takes off his glasses and drops the blanket he's wrapped in, appearing naked. "I'm beautiful!" he says. And he is. He starts rubbing his shoulders and chest, full of joy in the new body. Several sex scenes later, including an indistinct, creepy one he watches in "hell," Danny rejects the pact with the devil and is told by the cute neighbor that he's great just the way he is. The neighbor says he loves natural bodies and can't stand the vain West Hollywood jerks. Danny turns his studious wire rims to the camera for a close-up. The smile spills out, and he says, "Well, I'll be damned!" According to Darrell, the moderately awkward boy starring in that film was already a murderer.

Billy Houston "plays" bottom only once, a single scene in *Hip Hop Hunks*, which he tells me was the only time he was ever paid to bottom (the datum is important to him). He adds that he only did it because he was so attracted to the guy, a self-absorbed, bouncy, vacuous-looking, knit-cap-wearing "Tony Young," boyish but seemingly more Italian than Aryan. Darrell looks uncomfortable in the scene. When I ask whether it was particularly upsetting, given his feelings about "gay," he says that he was only self-conscious about that part of his body (his asshole). Something in his offhanded tone, though . . . an airy pleasantness completely stripped of feeling.

Like most careers in porn, Billy Houston's was short. He made six movies in two years and that was it. Despite the drugs, it was the high-water mark of his fortunes in California.

He'd arrived there from Houston around 1985, aged sixteen, as the guest of a Texas businessman at a West Hollywood hotel. Off hours he drifted down to Santa Monica Boulevard or to a hustler bar called Hunter's. For one admirer he spun the story that he was staying with his rich dad and was excruciatingly bored at the hotel. He was well-spoken enough, his looks angelic enough, to pull this off. He was taken home, photographed naked, paid nicely, sixty dollars for minimal sex. He says he had only two bad habits at the time: Diet Coke and Marlboro Lights. (But he'd killed in Houston, supposedly.) Soon he was living in West Hollywood and fell out of touch with his new friend.

Next time the Los Angeles friend saw him, four or five years later, Darrell was parked in front of a 7-Eleven on a new Honda Gold Wing (thirteen thousand dollars) dressed in leather with a leather cap, necklaces, diamonds on every finger, looking as gay as the day is long. "Looks like you found yourself a sugar daddy." Darrell just smiled. It was his first year in porn, 1990.

But in LA Darrell was also Richie Rich, a different person, not Lynn his hustler self, or Billy his porn self. Richie Rich hung out with skinheads who would have beaten or killed the other two. With the skinheads, he was always in a state of repressed ecstasy, thrilled by the crime, longing, brutality, and by the big falsehood itself. As usual, he distracted the others with shocking craziness. He out-hated the haters.

As he describes it now, each member of the skinhead gang had his lick. One taught them how to steal the empty video boxes from Blockbuster stores. A Chinese counterfeiter would buy them to dress up his own products. The boys (they really were boys, ranging from thirteen to twenty-one at most) stole mail and sold it to identity thieves or washed the ink off checks with methyl ethyl ketone and rewrote and cashed them using fake identities. Another lick was stealing concrete statues and huge urn planters. You had to lift the heavy planters, tree, soil, and all, straight up off the rebar that kept them in place. You dumped the prize in a stolen car, a puddle jumper good for one night, and took it to a very nice Mexican lady who'd buy every one and didn't mind being woken at four a.m. as long as you always came to her first. A dangerous but favorite lick was robbing the crack dealers on Crenshaw Boulevard, not a skinhead-friendly part of town. Gang members would pretend to be buyers (though crack was considered a "black drug," and they never touched it). When a dealer unwarily leaned in through the car window, his hand full of rocks, they'd knock it empty and peel out firing a shot over the man's head in parting. Afterward they combed the car for every last piece of crack and traded it for heroin, speed, pot, or cash. It didn't always work. Once they were crazy enough to try it with the gas gauge reading E and simply lucked out. Like the barbarous raiding parties in Tacitus's *Germania*, they robbed partly for the thrill, the story, for bragging rights in front of the youngest recruits.

On Saturdays they headed over to LA's largely Jewish

Fairfax neighborhood. The swastikas they'd spray-painted on the synagogues the night before were disappointingly already cleaned up, but they'd walk four or five abreast on the sidewalk, tattoos on display, talking racist trash and forcing Sabbath-goers to walk around them. Often they got violent. It was—perverse as it sounds—a joyous time. Joyous from within the gang, obviously. They were spreading terror. From my insular, nonviolent America, I rebelled at believing Darrell's stories for a long time.

Tentative as a mating black widow, Darrell now and then managed the seduction of a brother. After which, profound silence. Or he'd inveigle one to come with him to Santa Monica Boulevard to get a blow job for cash. After which, silence. Darrell himself had to be careful he wasn't flush with cash in too obvious a pattern. But money vanished like steam. Sometimes he was reduced to squatting with the gang.

That old client of his saw him again after a long break. It was near the notorious Okie Dog, a hustler and lowlife hangout. Lovely as ever, Darrell was in a wheelchair now. He explained that he'd developed diabetes. The client remembers taking him home, lifting him—a pornographic deposition of Christ—from wheelchair to bed, and having unforgettably tender sex (for money) with the angelic, wicked, damaged, diabetic boy.

Years later, after Steve Domer's and Bradley Qualls's murders, the same client nerved himself to visit Darrell in prison and worriedly asked whether the inmate was getting his insulin. Darrell chuckled and explained that he'd lied. He'd only needed the wheelchair after ruining his legs with drugs. He'd been hunting obscure veins to use for shooting meth.

When I visited a few months later and asked him again, Darrell smiled and told me, no, he'd lied again. The wheelchair was a scam from start to finish. No diabetes, no drugs either. One day he just decided he didn't want to walk anymore.

He liked the sympathy. He loved getting people to wheel him around. It lasted the better part of sixteen months. "Some of it," he admits, "was I thought they wouldn't be as likely to arrest a poor guy in a wheelchair for dealing drugs." That theory didn't pan out. He spent six months in the LA County jail, all the while pretending he was unable to walk. After the big-money years in porn and running a phony "agency" that had "Billy Houston" as its principal whore, Darrell was sliding into unglamorous drugs and crime, and soon he'd be tossed back to the plains of Oklahoma for good.

The truth, as you can see, becomes uncertain. There are old lies. Why did he need the wheelchair? There are self-confessed problems with memory, because he did take so many drugs. There may be a natural boastfulness now as he looks back from the monotony of prison, even a twisted pride in how awful he was. To hear him tell it, he was already a killer as a boy in LA and he killed again once he was there. I find it hard to believe. But I wouldn't peg him for a killer now, either. I've had to examine the truth ceaselessly while speaking with Darrell and writing about him.

There was talk about making a movie of his life. An interested filmmaker visited Darrell in prison. When I interviewed the filmmaker later about their meeting he described a Darrell I don't recognize. He says Darrell was incredibly scary, boasted about a fight with his cellmate

("I wiped the floor with him"), and claimed he'd committed his first murder as a kid in Houston. Asked to prove
himself to the skinheads there, he was handed a gun and
casually shot the next black guy to drive past.

The episodes of prison violence appear to be true. Darrell has told me about three bloody fights with three different cellmates. (About one he says, "I swear I wasn't leading
him on.") After each fight, he's left happily alone in the cell
until the next cellie (they're usually older, around fifty) is
brought in and, to use Darrell's word, "trained." Darrell
describes himself as autocratic and obsessive. He struggles
to control his bulimia, a lifelong problem. A screwup with
his laundry is completely unsettling to him. He rises at five
and likes to keep to a rigid schedule of TV shows (*Ellen*, *The
Price Is Right*, and, above all, Nascar), which keep anxiety at
bay.

I have a slightly girly/tyrannical vision of Darrell, so the
filmmaker's description is confusing. Most alarming, the
filmmaker says Darrell has lied to everyone about something crucial. After hearing my version of this story, the
filmmaker says in a low, disturbed tone of voice that Darrell told him that he (Darrell) had killed Steve Domer, not
Brad. That would change everything. I immediately have a
suspicion, though. The filmmaker is straight.

The first chance I get, I ask Darrell whether he got his
back up when he met the filmmaker because the man was
straight. Did he try impress him even to the point of appearing scary or unbalanced? Darrell says, "You are probably right about me being a little defensive where [he]
is concerned. I can be ME with you." This is important.
His behavior during that visit must have been convincing.
Someone familiar with actors and performances bought it

(considering he really is a killer, there's probably madness in Darrell's method). Here was a hint of Charles Manson, after all. More to the point, it was the blurry reflection of the "crazy, raging" Darrell that I have such a hard time visualizing. Darrell doesn't try to scare me. With a consistent love of regalia he asks me to send him the rainbow flag and pink triangle of his new "gang."

I do sometimes get the feeling that Darrell's holding back or even lying. He told me he didn't remember discovering his father's body in the chicken coop. "I know they say that, but I don't remember it," he once said to me with a strange, light finality. His tone made me think the story was either true and he didn't want to talk about it or an old lie still floating around, and he believed I might catch him in it. It would seem a difficult thing to forget.

Despite Darrell's steady and convincing frankness, doubts come up. Lies or reticences blur into the possibility that he simply doesn't remember things or understand himself. He can't possibly be as chipper about life without parole as he appears. In prison, Darrell sounds personable and upbeat, like a limo driver or a hustler trying to make a cheery first impression. He smiles readily. He flicks very long dark hair from his cheek with his good hand. He shows me the floppy left hand: "Poetic justice." When he pins the telephone handset between his ear and shoulder, his head is fixed at an endearing angle. He clearly wants to be liked and boasts, "They love me in here!" He stands and lifts his shirt to show the old tattoos he'd like to cover up. Since he isn't allowed the privilege of "contact visits" (his security level and the fights), you can only see him through a very blurry CCTV. The camera is slightly askew. The tattoos don't show up well. Making light of the prison indignity of protective custody (his life really is in danger from skinheads, and he's been afraid to go into the yard for a long time), he says happily, "In California it was considered bad, but everyone seems to do it here. It's like the thing to do."

With the usual hitches—my shirt snaps set off the metal detector—I'm let into the large visiting room through an entryway they keep at an elevated air pressure so the doors will always slam closed. The locks at either end open with a wheezy thud. Prisoners who are allowed contact visits are released into this room. Their families or girlfriends are already milling around or fussing with babies or reserving the too few chairs with a deft high school lunchroom sense of purpose. They stock up on junk food for the visit from the wall of snack machines. Everything but a roll of quarters has to be left in visitors' lockers outside. (This is a for-profit prison!) At the center of all the commotion a few corrections officers lounge at a desk.

The CCTVs, about six or eight of them, not all working, hang along the back wall opposite the snack machines. Voices are hard to make out through the balky phone system. The hubbub behind my back is distracting. Darrell now and then twiddles his fingers to wave over my shoulder at a wide-eyed three-year-old black girl in beaded braids. I smile, but if it's for my benefit it's wasted effort. I know that friendliness, even intimacy, is not the opposite of racism. In the lives of certain people, racism is like the morning fog, here and gone, always possible under the right conditions. Even if they wish it weren't so, it's become a phenomenon of their natures.

Almost too readily he says, "I've done such really awful, awful things." He seems more or less earnest. But he won't talk about the other possible murders (except to claim they happened both in Houston and California), because the CCTV records everything. "I really don't want the death penalty . . . Oh there now! I shouldn't be thinking of me. I should be thinking about those other people."

When I press him about how events escalated the night of Steve Domer's murder, he's quick to agree to my understanding of things. "Right, Brad and me were like always trying to outdo each other. It was a constant competition."

"But you came out on top in the end."

He bows his head at my irony, and the long hair screens the faintest of smiles, and he gently scolds me, "Oh, that's terrible. You're terrible."

5

A PRETTY MOUTH

Some men, straight or deeply closeted, cling to an outlandish horror that homosexuality is capable of destroying their identity or their soul. There's prison rape, and there's prison rape. One is real, a devastating assault. The other is a fantasy, a source of giggly discomfort and bad jokes. Surprisingly, the straight guy's horror is often more closely related to the silly fantasy than it is to the reality.

The 1970s, when popular culture was a little more serious-minded, was a particularly rich time for macho folklore to explore the creepy idea of being unmanned. The overblown Leon Uris novel *QB VII*, published in 1970, introduced a world-famous violinist turned into a "eunuch" by a Nazi doctor. Sam Peckinpah's brilliant *Straw Dogs*, ending with a sort of masculinity apocalypse, appeared in 1971. James Dickey's book *Deliverance* came out in 1970, and the film followed in 1972. Lines from it, "He got a real pretty mouth, ain't he?" and "I bet you can squeal like a pig. Weeeeeee!" soon rivaled dropping a bar of soap in the prison shower for heart-in-mouth snickers. James Clavell published his macho bodice-ripper *Shōgun* in 1975. That book is a parade of weird masculine fantasies including a strange scene of humiliation by being pissed on and glimpses of pederasty meant to cause shivers. In 1978 Oliver Stone gave us the screenplay for the male-rape "classic" *Midnight Ex-*

press, based on Billy Hayes's 1977 book. And somewhere in those years an aged John Huston appeared on the *Merv Griffin Show* and offered with his gravelly chuckle that he'd like his tombstone to read that he'd tried everything except sex with another man. One man's horror was another man's fantasy. Both were unreal.

For much longer than there have been superheroes and sidekicks, there have been stories that straight men find gripping and gay men find erotic or ridiculous. Modern awareness of homosexuality hasn't done away with it. A highly regarded journalist told me a story he'd heard from "intelligence sources" in Washington. A terror suspect was being tracked by drone while crossing a Middle Eastern waste in a Mercedes. A roomful of military men at an intelligence center somewhere in the United States monitored a live video feed of the action. Dumbfounded and horrified, they watched as the Mercedes stopped abruptly and two people got out. The suspect bent his driver over the hood of the car and started fucking him. Gravely, the watchers in the room called in a missile strike and blew the two Arabs up. There are infinite reasons to be skeptical about this story, and it was told to me with that in mind, but who cares? As a "story" it's pure James Clavell, and its currency— that it trickled down to me—says a lot about macho orientalism in government and journalistic circles.

Feminists are right when they distinguish between rape (an act of violence) and sex. To men this often isn't obvious without a moment of thought. But the same distinction exists between the two ways people think about sex between men. There's the "horror" version, a struggle, a contest, an act of violence. And then there's just sex, the helpless, compulsive act typical of human beings and other animals. The same genital instruments are used, so rape (or struggle) and sex look almost the same, and, of course, we muddy everything with our natural sense of play and metaphor. But the difference in desire and intent is vast, as big as the difference between putting a hammer to a nail and wanting to use one on a skull. We don't call both of these just "hammering."

James Dickey's "Mountain Man" is a character of barbaric masculinity who might turn any man into a "woman," which means, in macho parlance—and it's stunning how little-examined this definition remains—weak, dependent, owned, dominated. This is a masculine fantasy of struggle that couldn't be further from real homosexuality. But it allows unreflective straight men (and many women and gay people!) to categorize gay men as the losers in a metaphorical contest of masculinity. Many people and cultures secretly believe that "topness/maleness" and "bottomness/femaleness" are unified characteristics more fundamental than sexuality and, consequently, that the only truly gay men are the passive ones—male women, basically.

Straight men don't believe they "fear" gay men as the word "homophobia" implies. I've even heard some "out" homophobes complain about the word because of this supposed inaccuracy. They want to be clear that they're scornful, dismissive, contemptuous—not afraid—of gay men. If anything, they find lesbians more formidable. Mountain-man-uality might provoke an authentic fear, but that's something else, not gay.

Darrell Madden exhibited this thinking in an extreme, even pathological form. Though he was the rare double agent that "gay panic" stories seem to beg for, he also illustrated two other recurring images in masculine violence.

One is a racist-skinhead-backwoods-hick character that seems to be a cousin to Dickey's Mountain Man. The second is organization or gang behavior, the state of mind that allows someone to call a murder a "mission."

A killing back in 1999 involved a racist with none of Madden's changeableness or flair for performance. Comparing that case to Steve Domer's murder is interesting, because Billy Jack Gaither was similar in some ways to the Oklahoma man. And his killer was something of a youthful Mountain Man.

Gaither, from Sylacauga, Alabama, was a gawky gentle giant. He was known for his instinctive kindness, goofy grins, intense family loyalty (he lived with his parents), and small-town notions of propriety. Like Sylacauga's most famous son, Jim Nabors, Gaither went to Sylacauga High School and sang in his church choir.

Billy Jack never told his parents, Lois and Marion, that he was gay. Nor did he tell them he wasn't gay. His parents were of Nabors's generation, and because this was Sylacauga, you could leave it at that. It wasn't necessarily a case of Southern hypocrisy. Perhaps Billy was neither ashamed nor old-fashioned. Maybe the life he lived in Sylacauga was something modern and complex, like quantum mechanical superposition, gay and not gay at the same time.

Monday through Friday Billy Jack drove down to Alexander City where he worked for Russell Athletic, a big maker of the not-too-stylish clothes they issue in high school PE classes. He wasn't making a fortune, but he always had beer money. He could put a little aside and still afford nights out, sharp clothes and cowboy boots, a gold chain, a pricey haircut to offset his homeliness.

Evenings he'd swan into the Tavern, a roadhouse on

Route 280's commercial strip (the Jim Nabors Highway). I visited the place much later. A couple of lonely mic stands and a junked beer sign sat on a tiny stage toward the rear of the Tavern's single barnlike room. Twenty cheap black tables looked like they'd been set up for a chess tournament, except cigarette burns crawled over the tabletops and black leatherette upholstery like tent caterpillars.

Billy Jack met his killer here. This was Billy Jack's closeted, local hangout. He went to Birmingham to "be gay." But he may have had a sly sexual MO even here. After the murder, a man in the Coosa County Jail claimed he'd once gotten a long, odd stare from Billy Jack, and later found a yellow Post-it on his car in the parking lot: *For a blow job, call Billy Jack*, along with a phone number.

Now, that story was told to me by Billy Jack's murderer, so take it for what it's worth. At first the killer sounded reluctant to tell me, as if hesitating to defame the man he'd killed. He warmed up after a while and also told me that before burning Billy's car he'd found a Post-it pad inside with five or six sheets prewritten with the same message. He complained that Billy's religiosity had been exaggerated after his death. "I know cause he was driving me around on Sundays. He wasn't the saint they made out." None of this Post-it pickup or Sunday-driving behavior strikes me as remotely "bad," even if his murderer thinks I'll disapprove or disapproves himself. Probably the sourness comes out because he can't dismiss the larger, and probably painful, truth of Billy's charm and generosity toward him.

In the winter of 1999 Gaither started giving rides to a new bar friend from the Tavern, a thuggish twenty-five-year-old named Steve Mullins. They didn't talk much, and Billy didn't tell Mullins anything about being gay. Mullins wasn't the type. Behind the boy's countrified, half-comprehending face, shaved head, and goatee, Billy may have perceived a deeply rooted anger and opted to be cautious.

On the web of his right thumb and forefinger Mullins had a crude tattoo of the same runic *Schutzstaffel* double lightning bolt that Darrell Madden wore on his neck. Mullins had gotten his in prison too. He'd done two and a half years for the burglary of a dentist's office and forgery. Recently a bench warrant had been issued for him in Talladega County after he'd blown off a court appearance on a drunk driving charge. If he were spotted in Sylacauga he could be arrested. It was safer to lay low and let someone else do the driving. If Mullins needed a ride to Dollar General, for example, he'd call Billy Jack. He says others, as well—women—chauffeured him to the grocery store. Mullins wasn't shy about using people. But he tells me he and Billy Jack traveled in different circles and didn't like to be seen together. They didn't know one another's last name.

Steve's life was a mess just then. There was the bench warrant. He had no car, no job. Since prison he'd been living with Randall Jones ten miles outside Sylacauga. The only person who lifted his spirits, the only one who admired him, the only one he trusted, was Randall Jones's half brother Charlesy Butler. Charlesy lived with his father, Charles Sr., on Ricks Lane, which was on the other side of Sylacauga, past where East Third Street crosses the railroad tracks. (East Third turns into the Millerville Highway then runs up through the Talladega National Forest.)

Twenty-one-year-old Charlesy idolized Steve. In Steve, Charlesy found a guy who didn't back down from confrontation. Steve had the balls to walk around town in a white-power T-shirt, pissing off the Baptists, the earnest New South high school kids, the glad-handing businesspeople, the antique store faggots, basically everyone. If a black guy happened to come into the Tavern, Steve would sit at the next table and loudly start in on "nigger" this and "nigger-lover" that. You'd watch the black guy's face go hard and his insides turn to water. It wasn't something anybody saw or expected anymore, even in the Deep South.

Charlesy did construction grunt work like laying tar-paper shingles or mounting drywall for somebody's new family room. (The gleaming white gypsum board he used had its origin in a prehistoric reef on that very spot—the famous Sylacauga marble formation.) He was small, very small, only five-three and 120 pounds. He had red-blond hair and the beardless, gypsum-white face of an angel. His large eyes appeared strangely flat, as if they weren't set in his face so much as painted on, a sort of Celtic Fayum portrait. Steve's interest in Charlesy was obvious. Who doesn't like to have a follower? If the whole world thinks you're trash, aren't you drawn to the one person who treats you like a king?

The story is basically about Charlesy and Steve, Steve and Billy Jack. It's easy to imagine the minimalist conversations these two different pairs of friends would have had, full of drawled *uh-huhs* and *mm-hmms*. But in both cases a lot was being held back, important things weren't getting across. Steve and Charlesy had a sort of superhero and sidekick relationship. With Billy Jack there were sexual undertones. But—everything will turn on this—Steve insists he had no idea that Billy Jack was gay.

I've visited, and I can picture Billy Jack driving Steve back from Dollar General. They pass the hamlet of Gantt's

Quarry on the Sylacauga Fayetteville Highway. On the left is the old Alabama marble quarry. To the right a chestnut foal lopes up a rocky hillside pasture toward its mother. The sunbathed grass is cropped so close it looks like moth-eaten felt. They pull up to Randall Jones's white trailer amid soaring cottonwoods on Cedar Creek Circle. Here, cheap houses have been built along the shores of the dammed Coosa River. This part of Fayetteville is a hunting/fishing/boating sort of a place.

Under the nonverbal play of Billy Jack's imagined relationship with him, the angry Steve must have loitered like the shadow of a gar under the surface of the Coosa. Mullins tells me it happened like this: One day they were on the phone together and completely out of the blue Billy Jack said, "'I want to suck your dick.' I was like, 'Huh?' He says it again, 'I want to suck your dick.'" Invisibly, Mullins's immense hatred slewed toward the other man like the gar drifting in to strike. He says he was so shocked the first thing he thought was, *I gotta kill you*. The key was the shock, the surprise, the sneaky-seeming unexpectedness, not just the idea of homosexuality. That becomes clear later.

But how could a mere surprise affect someone so deeply? Mullins says he immediately started telling people he was going to kill Billy Jack. It was a matter of honor. "I told a LOT of people. I told them Billy was a secret fag. One said, 'You gotta do it alone.'" Others advised just beating him up. "I talked about it for weeks." He says now that Randall Jones and Preston, another of Charlesy's brothers, had a gay friend and that "gay" was no big deal for any of them (except Charlesy himself). It was something about the surprise. I want to say, perhaps, "uppityness" too.

Mullins was more explosive than anyone knew, more

than he knew himself. Somehow he'd become a kind of kid Mountain Man, though he hadn't been raised that way. He recites for me his mother's set of inflexible rules: "Don't have no friends who are black, who live in trailers, who have tattoos, who have single moms, who drive motorcycles." But Mullins also says he was constantly depressed as a child and started drinking at ten, smoking pot at twelve or thirteen. At around sixteen, he ran away from home after a fight. His mom shouted, "Don't take nothing with you!"

He says he started living in the "projects" with two other white guys. Everyone else there was black. He had black girlfriends and worked with a black drug dealer. But the racism he'd grown up with must have been intense, because in prison later he remembers feeling a repulsion for black inmates. Even African traits like black curly hair caused him to drift into a sick fantasy of splitting the black man's head open with an ax.

He tells me about one elaborate daydream he and a friend spun about murdering "a minority." The fantasy is horrifying and prefigures, in a few details and by many years, the murder of Billy Jack Gaither. It's as if that murder were somehow preexistent, awaiting the slightest jar to set it in motion.

"It was going to be a crackhead," Mullins tells me. "A nigger, a Mexican. We didn't even know any fags." He and his friend would trick the victim into a car, drive him to a secluded place, chain him to a low branch, and steady his feet with weights somehow. They'd pile tires underneath and douse them with gasoline, maybe make the guy swallow some, and then light him on fire. It was all about the fire. (I can't help being reminded of Darrell Madden and Brad Qualls verbally rehearsing their murder of Steve

Domer. But while the charming Madden can recount every horror fluently, the rumbling, dangerous-seeming Mullins is full of awkwardness and hesitation as he relates his story. I have the feeling there was even more to this fantasy than he can bring himself to tell me.)

On February 19, a Friday, at 8:12 in the morning, Steve phoned Charlesy Butler. Steve claims in one interview that he woke up that morning and the dire act was simply there, in his mind, ready to happen. "I just woke up and knew." To me he adds, "I went through the day like a well-oiled machine."

It had been drizzly on and off for three days. By midday the temperature rose to the upper fifties. The radio said it would finally clear overnight. Steve called Charlesy again at four in the afternoon. They talked. Mullins says both calls were about the murder. Immediately afterward, Steve called Billy Jack. Billy was at work in Alexander City. They talked about doing something that evening.

The events leading up to the murder are clear except for a crucial disagreement. Mullins says he talked about his plan to Charlesy and to "a lot" of people in the weeks before the crime. Charlesy denies it. (Wider knowledge about the coming murder has never been suspected.)

That evening Billy Jack swung by Cedar Creek Circle to pick up Steve Mullins. He drove a subcompact with dull purple metallic paint. He was carrying a six-pack of Bud Light. At about eight thirty p.m. the two men pulled into the Tavern parking lot. Billy went in to collect twenty dollars someone had borrowed and was inside almost an hour. From the Tavern, they drove to a place called the Frame. This time Steve went in and Billy Jack waited in the car. Steve found Charlesy inside playing pool. Charlesy and his father had come there straight from work in Birmingham (Charlesy was learning his father's trade, crane operator). The boy needed to wash and change.

Billy drove them both out East Third Street across the Norfolk Southern tracks. He passed his own church on the right, Eastside Baptist, a tidy modern brick building with a skinny, prefab white steeple. As promised the weather was clearing. They were already in the Talladega National Forest. East Third had become the Millerville Highway. Up here, in the woods to the left, were Ricks Lane and Charles Sr.'s place.

Mullins tells me he and Charlesy talked about the murder again in the house while Billy Jack waited outside. He says he casually mentioned a three-way to Billy as he got back into the car. Charlesy knew a quiet spot by the watersheds nearby, a boat launch. What locals called the "watersheds" were a series of little lakes, picturesque basins slotted amongst the hills of the national forest. An access road to Lake Victoria and Little Wills Lake was only a mile or so farther along the Millerville Highway.

Here, versions of the story diverge. This is how Mullins tells it: At the boat launch Charlesy stepped aside to pee. Billy Jack got out, took off his glasses, and came around behind the car. Steve joined him. Hands in the pouch of his white sweatshirt, Steve fingered an ordinary pocketknife with a black plastic handle. He pried open the three-inch blade with his thumbnail. He shook the knife from his sweatshirt pouch, pushed Billy to his knees from behind, reached around, and cut his throat. ("He was watching Charlesy take a leak. It was the right time. It pissed me off," he said later.) He stabbed Billy twice in the back.

He forced Billy into the rear well of the hatchback. It

doesn't make any difference, of course, but he points out to me that it wasn't the "trunk" that was reported everywhere. There was "just a flap cover. That car was very small. Not much bigger than a bed," he says, choosing an odd metaphor. They headed back to Cedar Creek Circle where Mullins had some things prepared. He tells me, "Billy came to and pleaded for his life" from the hatchback well. "He said, 'Come on, I won't tell anybody.' I said, 'You won't tell nobody you got your throat slit ear to ear? Hah. I gotta kill you. You're gonna die.' After that he got quiet."

In fact, Steve and Charlesy thought Billy Jack was probably dead by the time they got to Cedar Creek Circle and loaded up the car with what they needed. I ask Mullins about his preparations. He says old tires, kerosene, and matches just happened to be at the trailer, but he'd bought an ax handle specially. He recalls he also had a cooler with phone cord in it, and maybe some duct tape, in case they had to tie Billy up.

They took a shortcut locals call One-Minute Road down to Talladega Springs. They turned away from Sylacauga on the main road. Just over the line in Coosa County, they crossed a small river, Peckerwood Creek, and took a sharp left onto a dirt road running along the river and into the woods. They drove to a junk-strewn turnaround next to the concrete footing of an older bridge, long gone.

While Charlesy dragged the tires ten feet away and got them burning, Steve began to wrestle Billy Jack from the car. He turned away for a moment and felt himself pushed from behind. He tripped forward over the riverbank, falling ten feet into the water. He let the splash go quiet. Wet from head to toe, he found his footing and stood in the knee-deep water. Atop the bank he could hear a car door open, the awkward bumping of the ax handle against metal and—a bit farther off—leafy thudding: Charlesy was high-tailing it away through the woods. Steve scrambled up the riverbank.

Billy Jack had crawled into the front seat of the car and was clutching the ax handle. "I told him he wasn't going nowhere cause I had the keys in my pocket." Wet, angry, Steve yanked Billy Jack from the car and jerked the ax handle from his hand. He brought it down on Billy's head or face with all his strength. He brought the ax handle down again. He continued with chorelike regularity. Finally, he called Charlesy back.

Together the boys dragged the body onto the tires. They doused it with kerosene and the flames leaped up. They lobbed the red jug, the ax handle, and Steve's white sweatshirt onto the fire. Then they waited till they were sure the body was burning, about five minutes. It was fire enough to fulfill Mullins's fantasy. They returned to Cedar Creek Circle. After borrowing Randall Jones's car and burning Billy's, after cleaning up and going for a final beer together at Southern Station on Route 280, Steve dropped Charlesy off at Ricks Lane around three a.m. Charlesy immediately woke Charles Sr. and said, "We killed a guy." He wept. "Daddy, we kicked a queer's ass."

On Monday, the first day of March, Charlesy Butler was picked up. His daddy had told his own friend, Joey Breedlove, about the killing. After the Gaithers held Billy's funeral, Breedlove went to the police. Steve was soon arrested. In a statement to the Coosa County sheriff he confessed in calm, inarticulate detail. He'd killed Billy Jack because Billy was gay and for his money. He said he and Charlesy had plotted "getting rid" of Billy for a couple of weeks, ever since Billy had insulted Steve by asking to give him a blow job. He'd conspired with Charlesy, because he knew Charlesy also hated queers. He thought he could trust the younger boy. To me, Mullins has added the unverifiable detail that Charlesy once said he'd been abused by a member of his own family. It was why he hated queers so much. I've written Charlesy in prison and gotten no response.

The news spread quickly. The story was picked up in the Atlanta paper, and the *New York Times* sent a reporter, David Firestone, to Sylacauga. This was that boom year for hate murder, 1998–1999. Less than five months earlier Matthew Shepard had been killed. Then there'd been James Byrd Jr., whom newspapers reflexively described as "the black man who was dragged to his death in Texas." Billy Jack was lumped together with the other two. It was done without malice but with the same attention-grabbing logic that sold the Three Tenors to people who cared nothing about opera.

Locals hated how their perfectly modern small city came off sounding like an evil Mayberry RFD. Reporters pronounced the words "small town" ghoulishly on air. TV producers loved shots of the weedy Norfolk Southern tracks. A train whistle would moan behind the voice-over, "Sylacauga is the kind of place where every family keeps at least a few chickens." Hardly. The Firestone article appeared Saturday, March 6, two weeks after the murder. It reported that "[t]he murder is being called another signpost of hate, like the deaths of Matthew Shepard, killed in Wyoming last year because he was gay, and James Byrd Jr., the black man dragged to his death behind a truck last year in Jasper, Texas."

The previous day the Clinton White House published a presidential statement about the murder, and two ministers and an Episcopal layman from Boston trudged out to the bridge footing by Peckerwood Creek with several reporters in tow. The ministers prayed and laid four daffodils on the spot where Billy's body had been burned. Members of Fred Phelps's despicable family-run Westboro Baptist Church came from Topeka, Kansas, to protest against a candlelight vigil held in Sylacauga on March 8. Phelps's daughter Rebekah, then eleven, held a sign reading, *Gaither in Hell*.

In news lingo the big "get" was Mullins. The prize went to Connie Chung of the ABC News program *20/20*. Her interview wasn't broadcast till December, well after Steve and Charlesy had both been imprisoned for life. That gave her short piece a nice sense of closure.

Chung narrates with tabloid gusto: ". . . They left the scene of their evil inferno . . ." Then Steve is shown coming through a Kilby prison hallway, clean-shaven now, wearing an orange jumpsuit. His forearms are chained to a restraint around his waist, his wrists handcuffed for good measure. The camera zooms in on the SS tattoo on his hand.

Chung dominates the interview. Perhaps her combative, feeling manner is an effective interview technique precisely because it's so unsettling. She gets Mullins to cry cinematic tears, to which she reacts with an almost imperceptible, righteous shaking of her head and pursing of her lips. She's undoubtedly correct when she narrates, "The tears [he and Charlesy] shed are not for their victim but for their own bleak futures." Chung's garish personality all but eclipses Steve's hollow voice and *Yes, ma'am*s.

Steve tries to explain that while he was beating Billy

Jack to death, "It wasn't me. It was like it was another person. Someone else inside me."

Chung shoots back: "How can you say it was someone else? Because in fact you were thinking about it and you were intending to kill him . . . It's obvious . . . You were a skinhead and you were a neo-Nazi and that is all about you. So that's who you were."

"Guess so."

When asked if he felt remorse, Steve says, "Yes, for a couple days. Then I took my Bible and I prayed and asked for forgiveness." Rigidly Steve claims that God has forgiven him, but that Billy is in hell because he was homosexual. "It's in the New Testament. I could show you where if I had a Bible."

"Why would God forgive you?" Chung asks incredulously. She seems more aggravated than intrigued by Steve's self-protective stubbornness.

Steve stopped giving interviews after that. (I wondered if it hadn't been the tears—thinking that he came off weak. But he's told me he never saw the show and that he stopped talking "mostly" because he'd promised the producer an exclusive.) The PBS show *Frontline* was also preparing a documentary and had to borrow some of ABC's footage when Steve wouldn't speak to them.

Before hearing his oddly credible claim about keeping the promise of an exclusive, I'd also wondered whether Mullins stopped talking because he didn't want to be asked about a piece of the story that ABC omitted. Mullins had been to a "gay party" in nearby Anniston once. He'd attended with someone named Jimmy Lynn who claimed he'd performed oral sex on the future murderer. This came out at trial. Did the case involve another gay secret agent, another Darrell Madden ten years before the fact? It doesn't seem possible that ABC missed this (the "gay" testimony was given four months before their episode of *20/20*, "Murder Out of Hate," was broadcast), so one assumes they found the information too complicated to explain briefly, too charged for their audience, liable to reflect badly on Billy or to weaken their punchy gay-martyr plotline. Or simply distasteful.

Even the admirable *Frontline* couldn't resist using the information for shock effect. After the whole awful story has been told, Forrest Sawyer intones, "But Steve Mullins had a secret homosexual sex life."

Charlesy is interviewed by Sawyer. Crying freely, his red hair shorn, puffy (*Medication?* I wonder), he suggests that the lie about the Anniston party means Steve is less trustworthy than he, Charlesy, is. This is important because Charlesy and Steve don't agree about what happened the night Billy was murdered.

First, Charlesy claims there was no plan. He says he had no idea what was going to happen ahead of time. Steve and he never talked about "getting rid" of Billy. Nothing was said about murder that night or before. Nothing was said about luring Billy with a promise of sex. Charlesy himself, in a sense, was lured up there. In short, Steve was lying about everything.

According to Charlesy, Billy Jack first suggested a three-way at the boat launch by Lake Victoria. Insulted, he, Charlesy, kicked Billy to the ground. He kicked him several more times for good measure. His panicky anger assuaged, he walked off and took a leak. When he came back Steve had cut Billy's throat and stabbed him. Charlesy says he doesn't know why Steve did it, but in light of Steve's lies

. . . He trails off and lets us do the imagining. Charlesy has an air of tragic candidness. His life really has been ruined. The fact that Steve had gotten a blow job and might secretly be gay may strike Charlesy as a betrayal in retrospect. With what sounds like a straight guy's—or an inmate's—brutal Mountain Man view of homosexuality, Charlesy mumbles, "[Billy] didn't have no respect. It's not like I'm some gay tramp waiting to be cornholed by some prick." He pleads with Forrest Sawyer, "Would you like for a gay man to hit on you?"

Earnestly Sawyer replies, "I don't think I'd kick him."

Frontline seemed to find Charlesy's version plausible, but it's probably fiction.

Even if you're inclined to buy a panic story, a glance at the legal maneuvers surrounding his trial hints that Charlesy is lying. On March 4, the two boys were indicted. On June 4, Mullins pled guilty in return for life without parole. On August 2, Charlesy refused the same deal. He wanted to go ahead with a trial. On August 3, his trial began. His lawyer painted him as a foolish, volatile kid who came under the influence of a lying thug and secret homosexual—Mullins. Witnesses testified that Mullins went to a "gay party" and had oral sex with a man. But the story didn't sell. Or else Charlesy's actions immediately after the murder—helping to burn the body—were too unmitigating. On August 5, he was found guilty. Since the devout Gaither family opposed the death penalty, the prosecutor took that option off the table as he had with Mullins, and Charlesy Butler got life.

It's hard not to feel sorry for the kid, though he understands nothing. The gleeful punch line that he's probably getting fucked in prison—and deserves it—is about as funny as a gay murder by a creek named Peckerwood. With wilting discretion the *Frontline* website mentions that Charlesy talked of having to deal now with "prison sexuality." They leave it at that.

But sexuality is exactly what makes this story so interesting and so confusing. Billy Jack was a gay man passing for straight. Charlesy was a small, straight kid with, for lack of a better term, a pretty mouth. He may have been abused when he was younger. What about Mullins? I asked him. He told me he was "bisexual." He prefers women but lacking one will have sex with an effeminate man. He described the first time he had sex in prison in 1995 (four years before the murder). He leafed through *Hustler* magazine while someone gave him a blow job under a table. The second time—the only time outside of prison—was with Jimmy Lynn. Once. The Anniston party was mostly lesbians and he was there with a girl. It doesn't sound like a secret homosexual life. (Mullins is certain Billy Jack had never heard anything about Jimmy Lynn or the Anniston party.)

With his stress on effeminacy, I have an intuition Mullins is talking about bisexual *behavior*, not desire, so I ask about fantasies with guys. No. Was there any attraction to Charlesy? No. To Billy Jack? No. And I consult with a gay man from out of state who's befriended him since he was locked up and who agrees that Mullins seems basically straight. Our beliefs about innate sexuality don't trump everything, though. Mullin's description of himself is a reminder that opportunistic, or even chosen, sexuality is also real.

Mullins says he's had a lot of sex over the years since the killing. "It has to be with someone feminine. And some sort of attraction. I had a (black) prison wife whom I love and loved very much. He is now at home. He was the last person I was with a year ago." These days, if someone offers Mullins a blow job—he relates this to me lightly, apparently forgetting it was the original motive for murder—he begs off, saying he's retired. I ask an amazed question, and he specifies that *every* guy he's ever had sex with was black. That physical revulsion he experienced when younger takes on a stranger aspect. The "toppish," racist, mountain man Mullins is a far more convoluted being than our culture—at least in the persons of Connie Chung and Forrest Sawyer—wants to allow.

Earlier, I mentioned that the Oklahoma City killer, Darrell Madden, bore some racist or backwoods cultural resemblance to Steve Mullins. Madden's gang affiliation was the other standout aspect of his story. He kept calling the murder of Steve Domer "a mission." His word choice recalls the war-minded, militaristic Ben Williams. But where Williams's "mission" was social purification, Madden's involved gang initiation. Williams's object was religious/political, Madden's brotherly.

I went to the other side of the country, to Baltimore, to look at gang violence from another angle. This was a case of organized violence without the erotically charged subtext that Madden's personality gave his story. In a less tragic world, this case would have been an episode of school violence, a pantsing, literally, with everybody feeling ashamed and miserable afterward, but no more than that.

6

PARRISH, RAWLINGS, HOLLIS, AND FLYTHE, 2008

Randallstown, Maryland is one of those well-maintained middle-class suburbs, like Gary, Indiana, that over the past decades, without any fuss, has become almost entirely African American—more than eighty percent at last count. Regulation plastic garbage cans are left atilt at the curb in front of modest single-family houses. The cars are mostly Toyotas, though there's an Infiniti in one driveway and the occasional beater or Harley. Unmowed lawns are rare. The air of conformity is standard-issue suburban.

Older people might mistake the town for an enclave of Polish autoworkers, because, frankly, it looks like the kind of place blue-collar racists tried to keep black people *out* of in the bad old days. Instead, no one has to think about integration here at all. As if bookending a whites-only past, nearly every face you see is brown—an even higher percentage of African Americans than in Baltimore next door.[7]

Many of the families in Randallstown came here to get out of crime-ridden Baltimore. Shrinking since 1950, Baltimore is now hardly more than a borough of the Boston-to-Washington megalopolis I-95 ties together.

---

7. Of major US cities, Baltimore has a higher percentage of African Americans than any but Detroit and New Orleans.

Thirty thousand old houses are abandoned and boarded up. The reputations of Edgar Allan Poe and Frederick Douglass have faded equally. The city's new mythology has come from the TV show *The Wire*. To a visiting New Yorker (me), the crime-consciousness feels like a throwback to the 1970s. The local, alternative, free *City Paper* runs a roundup column called "Murder Ink." A recent issue's headline tally was, "Murders This Week: 6; This Year: 109."

Randallstown has little in common with *The Wire's* gangsta paradise of Section 8 housing, trashed row houses, and hyperalert but stoned-acting loiterers giving the four-fingers-down signal of dope dealers. In Randallstown the kids are good, though they mostly go to the not-so-good Randallstown High School. That sprawling brick pile couldn't be more suburban, set amid acres of parking lots and tennis courts and basketball courts and playing fields. Almost hiding the entrance, a windowless, modernist Martello tower juts out toward a parking lot. Against the tower's mass of brick, a banner of the school's mascot ram is almost lost. A corner of the banner has come away and flutters briskly to the shouting of a thousand kids.

At the end of the school day the buses have lined up in front of the school. Most kids mill around waiting for their ride, but a lot walk home: a threesome of fat girls, an undersized, bespectacled loner with an oversized backpack, a knot of seniors with a student-comedian shuffling backward on the sidewalk in front of them telling jokes. Within an hour or so, like a wave into sand, the shrilling crowd disappears completely into the suddenly quiet suburb.

Sometimes Michelle Parrish, in every way an ordinary mother, would come to this school to pick up her son Steven and his best friend Steven Hollis. She'd drive them to her place and the two Stevens would have a sleepover. Or else the boys would walk from school several blocks to the Hollis home on Bengal Road, and they'd spend the night there. They were pretty much inseparable best friends.

Parrish more was more handsome and gregarious. His nickname was "Scooby." Hollis's academic problems were somehow reflected in his face—he was an odd-looking kid. His nose, cheeks, and jaw jutted forward. The top part of his head was smaller and narrower. Attractive eyes receded under a strange, sharply V-shaped brow, a permanent frown that made him appear both uncomprehending and on the verge of anger. He'd had a blood disorder when he was born and was diagnosed with ADHD as a seven-year-old, but neither would account for that scarily tragic expression. Maybe it was why they called him "Loco."

In high school, a frustrated Loco discovered the one thing he excelled at, football. At six-one and 190 pounds, he was a good fit. Scooby encouraged him. As they got older the pair joined up with a whole band of school friends. Juan Flythe was "Woo." Jasiah Carroll was "Scrappie."

The boys found the Parrish place ideal for hanging out. Where the Hollises' small Bengal Road house—white with black shutters—was crowded in amongst other houses, the Parrish's place was in Gwynn Oaks Landing, a vast rental project of two-story tan brick townhomes. The homes came in eight- or ten-unit blocks arranged in simple patterns on short dead-end streets off a stretch of Essex Lane. The streets had cute names like Strawbridge Court and Cedar Park Court and Mountbatten Court. The Parrishes lived at 21 Thornhurst Court. Though all rental, the complex looked like a well-maintained condo project. A parklike barrier of woods and artful boulders separated

Essex Road from the townhomes and parking lots. Unseen, vigilant neighbors were everywhere.

But what made it such a good place for hanging out was that all those dead-end "Courts" and townhomes backed up against a dense patch of woods, heaven for kids to play in, to explore, to make out in, to get drunk or high in. 21 Thornhurst Court was all the way at the back where, right next to a garbage bin, a path opened into the woods.

The forest has a name only a mapmaker would know (Villa Nova Park), but it is just called "the woods." If you walk in past the garbage bin at the end of Thornhurst Court, you can go straight through brush down a steep ravine to Gwynns Falls Creek. Crossing the stream in a couple of hops, you can climb the even steeper far side of the ravine. Up there, trees and brush are suddenly replaced by lawns and gravestones, the more recent ones forlornly decorated with plastic flowers and burnt-out tea lights holding puddles of old rainwater like lachrymal vases. This is Woodlawn Cemetery, also a terrific place for a kid to play. Just the right mix of eeriness, emptiness, cranky groundskeepers, and a pond (a dammed stretch of the creek) almost too small for a huge, nearly tame flock of mallards. Idlers are always feeding them with crumbled bread.

If you turn sharply right from the garbage bin, you'll follow a path along the crest of the ravine's near side. This shortcut behind the townhomes of Gwynn Oaks Landing pops back out onto Essex Road where you can make a left on Windsor Mill Road. Down a hill is the area's main drag with a Royal Farms store (a local chain of gas stations/quickie marts) and the police station.

Idyll though all this appears for a boy whose family doesn't have a lot of money, when adolescence hits, and the shadow of Baltimore seems to inch closer, a boy's thoughts can turn to gangs, even in Randallstown. Even good kids give it some thought. The universal alarm that gang life inspires in places like Randallstown looks like power to a kid who's worried about disrespect. The all-diminishing mockery of high school can't touch gang members.

Still, compared to criminal Baltimore City types, these particular boys from surrounding Baltimore County might as well have been country bumpkins. How serious can a gang get in a suburb? Maybe it was more like a fraternity, an in-your-face version of the "Greek Life" some African Americans embrace in college. These guys, Loco, Woo, were on the football team, after all. What does this have to do with crime? Their interest in a gang had to be juvenile swagger, play. Unfortunately, the nature of play is always to mimic the real thing.

About to graduate from high school, the boys found part-time jobs. They had to. A storage center. A day labor agency. They were getting a glimpse of the life ahead of them. Scooby found work at a pharmacy on Liberty Road, one of the big streets radiating from downtown Baltimore. A gay guy named Jimmie worked there too. He was older, in his thirties, perhaps. Though Scooby wasn't bothered by a gay guy, the work was boring. Loco took a job as a cashier at a McDonald's. It wasn't exactly football and his permanent frown may have started to represent real surliness.

They all revered a slightly older guy with the street name "Murk" (Benjamin Wureh). And when they talked to him about forming a gang, he advised them, "You wanna make it real, you gotta go to Hood."

"Hood" was Timothy Rawlings Jr. He was four years

older than the two Stevens. He was much smaller as well, only five-nine and 157 pounds. He looked like a kid, an extremely grave kid. His hair was cropped short, no fancy dreads or cornrows or the gumball-sized twists Loco wore. His humorless charisma was just the kind to win young men over. Small as he was, he'd been the quarterback of the Parkville High School football team. He had a still, wild form of leadership, self-conscious of his power, forever poised, permanently insecure.

Real morality was probably invisible to a guy as focused as Hood. What took its place was ritual, rules, signs, the arcana of groups and obscure subgroups like FOE: "If you rep that FOE, you about Family Over Everything."

Hood's father was a career criminal with other things than family on his mind. Hood lived just inside the Baltimore city limits with his mother, Tereia Hawkins, who'd raised him alone. She was a long-time state employee, a corrections officer, ironically. A huge, slow woman, she had an air of long-suffering endurance. Under a smattering of unprofessional tattoos, her upper arms swung like wattles when she moved.

Once the boys hooked up with Hood, things changed quickly. They would be Bloods—that is, they'd side with the American archipelago of gangs who favor red and, along with the Crips, are one half of a modern underground version of the ancient Blues and Greens, the quasipolitical hippodrome fanatics who terrorized Constantinople. (Most old pictures of Scooby show him wearing a pregang blue bandanna, not the red one that became part of his gang wear and his last outfit.)

You couldn't just be a Blood. You kouldn't just start religiously avoiding the Crips' letter C when you texted your boyz. History and heraldry were involved. Most gang names hark back to an address, street, or neighborhood in Los Angeles where the Crips and Bloods got their start. That's where "Swans" came from, apparently. Under Hood the Randallstown boys would become "Family Swans 92" or the "92 Family Swans." Each gang member had a swan or the name tattooed on their shoulder or arm.

When Michelle and Steven Sr. saw the tattoos Scooby had gotten on his forearms, they were furious. Scooby's father, a large man with the weary manners of millions of American husbands, grumbled with repulsion and let his wife rail at their son. She was a sharp-tongued woman. But even she ran out of words eventually, and she threw up her hands and shook her head in bitter disappointment, a pot boiling dry though still on the flame.

Scooby was a charmer and tried explaining to his parents that, yes, it was a gang, but it didn't mean he was going to have to do anything bad or illegal. It was just group friendship. Like the one between him and Loco. Nothing different. His parents challenged him: how would it look when he went for a job? He promised, he swore, it was nothing bad, not the big deal they thought it was.

Other parents had the same reaction. But how do you confront an ever-more-remote and indifferent kid? Woo's (Juan Flythe's) father didn't even know what his son was up to until he found out from a cousin. She told him Juan was hanging out with a bad crowd. So Juan's father went to his own mother, Bercille, a tough, almost mannish woman with whom Juan was living at that point. Father and grandmother discussed it. Yet they couldn't do more than discuss and worry. They certainly weren't going to talk to the police about the boy they loved, though a judge later wished aloud, idly, that parents would do just that in gang cases.

The Parrishes, at any rate, regained a little hope after the initial shock. Scooby really was an endearing kid. He was about to graduate. He went off to driving school every day around four thirty, taking that shortcut through the woods. He'd applied for a UPS job. And he was thinking about Baltimore Community College.

May 25, 2008 was Scooby's eighteenth birthday. He was a senior, school was almost over, the weather was getting warmer, he was tight with the 92 Family Swans—things must have felt good.

He had friends over to 21 Thornhurst Court for a birthday party for himself. The inner circle came: Loco, of course, and Woo and some girls—the high school crowd. Murk came, but not Hood. This party may have seemed too suburban or kidlike to him. Or maybe he thought his absence would add to the mystique of leadership. Soon enough Scooby disappeared upstairs with his girlfriend. It was his birthday after all.

Downstairs the party continued. Why someone picked up Scooby's cell phone, which he'd left downstairs, isn't clear, but the lead detective on the case wonders whether the kids weren't searching for naked pictures of the girl-friend so they could razz the pair about it later.

Anyway, they clicked their way through Scooby's cell phone, and they did find a picture. It was a shot of Scooby's penis. That might have been good—funny and embarrassing enough—but the photo was part of a text exchange between Steven Parrish and Jimmie, the older gay guy who worked at the Liberty Road pharmacy. The exchange was humorous, if anything. As recalled by the same detective, it went something along the lines of:

Jimmie, u see wat I got here? U wishin huh?

I don see nuthin much. Dat all u got me fo ur bday?

U see it good enuf.

Nobody told Scooby what they'd seen on his phone; he was still busy upstairs. Apparently the bedroom tryst didn't seem significant compared to the queer texts. Loco and Woo became confused and angry. They left soon afterward. Maybe a faint, moblike outrage filled the air, because someone also stole the girlfriend's iPod before leaving.

"Gayness" in this story is all but ungraspable. Everyone says Scooby was straight. A lot of them insist on it more than seems decent (as if his murder would make sense otherwise). He did have girlfriends. And it's not uncommon for a straight boy to get a kick out of the attentions of a gay man.

Regardless, Loco and Woo were suddenly as angry about Scooby's sexual identity as Michelle had been about his gang identity. Why they reacted this way is hard to understand. In Loco's case I imagine he felt compromised himself. Young people think their reputations echo across the world. This could have been too great a blot. The whole world knew Scooby and he were best friends. The world knew about the sleepovers, knew they'd grown up together and shared an intimate loyalty to one another.

An additional driving issue may have had to do with football and the 92 Family Swans, not so much sudden discomfort about the gray area of male bonding as the idea that any team has to have a unified purpose, and certain kinds of individuality ruin that. Destruction of a weak link isn't destruction at all. It's fortifying, honorable, sanctioned.

Loco and Woo stewed through the 26th and most of the 27th before Woo finally said, "We gotta take it to Hood."

As Hood saw it, too many people had been at the party, too many people knew. And "gay," because of its aura of submission, meant weak. Hood felt in the abstract—on behalf of the 92 Family Swans—exactly as Loco felt for himself. How would it look? Family Over Everything. The F in FOE didn't mean family, of course, except in the Mafia sense. Only brutal, gangsta irony would make a sweet-sounding slogan into an acronym like FOE.

Scholars have written about scorn in ancient times for the bow as a combat weapon. It was used, but a feeling existed from at least as far back as Homer that there was something ignoble about the arrow's power to kill at a distance compared to hand-to-hand combat, which measured man against man. ("Archery is no test of a man's bravery. A man stands fast in his rank and faces without flinch the gashing of the quick spear." Euripides, *Heracles*.) The same unease recurs throughout the developmental history of weapons. Six-shooters got the moniker "equalizers" because they made size and strength nonissues. And the problem is with us right now in its most dramatic form ever, when joysticks in Florida control drones on the Afghan-Pakistan border.

This is relevant, because Hood was about to murder at a distance. The testimony from Florida is that killing at a distance isn't like a video game at all. It feels real. So Hood, this small, serious twenty-two-year-old, was probably going to feel the reality of it too, no matter how he played it. On May 28 he called a meeting.

His gang met him at the Mondawmin Mall. The mall is a huge, cheap bilevel structure with a gleaming all-white interior. You'd never guess it was actually the oldest enclosed mall in Baltimore, dating from 1956.[8] It's located on the rapid transit line halfway between Randallstown and Baltimore's Inner Harbor and has the usual complement of national chains, plus a check-cashing place, a wig store. A Pakistani-run jewelry shop sells stereotypical bling while outside guys hawk African-style tribal items. But the mall has a dangerous reputation. In some quarters it's spoken of as the kind of place white people might not want to go. And despite the security guards, I saw people buying dope in the men's room.

At the center of the mall is a huge skylit atrium. A glitzy spiral staircase swoops down from a second-level balcony over a circular reflecting pool. Shops line the upper level except right at the balcony, which serves as a sort of lounge. Against a sunny wall of plate-glass windows, overstuffed neo-Deco chairs have been arranged around square fake-leather-upholstered tables or footstools. When I was there, I watched what looked like idling gang members flounce en masse onto the lounge chairs. This is likely where the meeting took place. Besides Hood, at least Loco, Woo, Scrappie, Justin Inman, and Marc Miller were present. Others may have escaped mention.

At the meeting, it was made clear that Scooby, based on what was now "known" about him, was going to make the 92 Family Swans look weak or vulnerable. There had already been a few fights with Crips. Scooby himself had

---

8. The name was borrowed from Mondamin, the Indian corn god in Longfellow's "Song of Hiawatha," whom Hiawatha wrestles to death in a strange foreshadowing of Scooby's own death: "And before him breathless, lifeless,/Lay the youth, with hair disheveled,/Plumage torn, and garments tattered,/Dead he lay there in the sunset."

been involved in one or two, though they were more like schoolyard tussles than a gang war. Ultimately, the opinion of fellow Bloods may have been just as important.

Hood took all this seriously. It was his nature. Maybe he was really hoping to build a criminal enterprise someday. Maybe he was simply drinking down the experience of his own leadership in breathless gulps. Or running as fast as he could in his thoughts to remain out in front of the rest of them.

Loco was speaking about his closest friend, but he was looking at Hood, a boy quarterback wearing an expression as somber and unreadable as a lizard's. Hood was saying that they had to *do* something about this. These boys had been studying rules and rituals from the moment their gang was founded. Probably few of them dared offer more than grunts of assent when Hood gravely invoked some heartless rule. A law. He chose who would take care of it. He told them to get it done quickly.

On the 29th, the next day, a couple of people were warned to stay away from the Parrish place. Murk texted Justin Inman and told him not to go to Thornhurst Court that afternoon, even though Inman had been picked as one of the killers. "It is going to be hot over there. They are going to do that thing." Murk, who was older, may still have felt a glimmer of choice. For everyone else, choice had vanished.

It was Loco—Steven Hollis—and Woo—Juan Flythe—who went to Thornhust Court at around four thirty in the afternoon. Loco was seen approaching the Parrish place, where he'd spent so much of his childhood. He lingered by the black-painted metal door, set back like all the others in an arched recess. This was the time Scooby usually went to driving school, and he soon came out. He and Loco walked around the corner of the building toward the garbage bin and woods. Maybe Woo was in the woods already or joined them as they entered.

Woo and Loco later told a friend that they confronted Scooby about the picture and that he said he didn't want to talk about it. They dwelled on the fact that Scooby never denied the picture's implication. Loco supposedly grumbled, "We did what we had to do."

What Scooby said to them in the woods isn't known apart from the screamed half-sentence or two overheard by witnesses. The three boys got about halfway down the path, the shortcut that veers right. Whether they were arguing or sullen, whether Scooby was furious or embarrassed, he couldn't have been expecting what happened. Woo grabbed his friend and started cutting. Echoing Steve Mullins, the Alabama killer, Woo says he didn't feel quite present during the attack. Scooby was heard screaming, "Hey! Stop! Why you doing this to me . . . ? I didn't do nothing!" The pleading went on for a short while. Badly cut, Scooby broke away from Woo and hurtled toward Loco, who shoved his own knife into Scooby's chest, cutting the side of his heart.

Scooby fell. Loco and Woo now beat and kicked him. Woo says Loco was in a frenzy. He stomped on his best friend's neck, crushing the boy's windpipe. Either the cut to the heart or the crushed neck would have been fatal. But Scooby had over fifty cuts on his hands and head and body. It was about 4:50. The killers took their victim's cell phone, camera, and pocketknife. Woo says Loco also took Scooby's pants off—as if in ritual humiliation. The pants were never found, though Murk swears he later saw them and the phone at Woo's house. As a last gesture, either Loco or Woo laid a red bandanna over Scooby's face.

The killers made cell phone calls to fellow gang members at 4:55 and 4:56, probably before they left the woods. "It's done." At 5:02, Scrappie (Jasiah Carroll) texted: "So is he gone or wat?" Murk answered: "Shut da fuk up."

Fifteen or twenty minutes later, a neighborhood guy named Blaze came up the path from the opposite direction. He stopped. He ran the rest of the way to Gwynn Oaks Landing. He spotted a couple of girls he knew: "You wanna see Scooby's body? He's up in the woods!" A 911 call had been put in as soon as the screaming was heard. Not long after Blaze found the body, police arrived.

During those fifteen or twenty minutes, Loco and Woo must have walked the length of the shortcut and come out on Essex Road without running into Blaze. They later said they'd chucked their knives in one of the garbage bins. Loco and Woo kept walking to Windsor Mill Road, turned left, and strolled down the steep hill alongside busy traffic. They were probably bloodied, probably carrying a bloody pair of pants. They walked right past the police station to the parking lot of that Royal Farms store.

Meanwhile, Hood was driving around Baltimore in his gray Dodge Avenger (a sexy limited-edition model named, incredibly, "Stormtrooper"). In the bucket seat next to him sat Curtis McClean. Despite the huge wings tattooed across his back, McClean wasn't a member of the 92 Family Swans. ("That guy was so big he didn't have to bother about gangs," a detective later explained to me.) Hood got a phone call and told McClean, "I gotta pick my boys up." The agreed-upon spot was the Royal Farms store.

So there were four of them in the sporty Avenger. Presumably, team killing demands team debriefing or team congratulations. Not a happy slap on the butt so much as a grave, "You did what had to be done."

They drove downtown to the Bentalou-Smallwood neighborhood of southwest Baltimore. Christian Street is a drab-looking stretch of cheap old brick and clapboard town houses, several with fake stone siding. Dead quiet during the day, the street is home to a couple of bars. One, on the corner of Payson, has no sign except a neon *Open* in a tiny window. Across the intersection is a shabby, gray-painted place called Incognito. *Open Seven Days* and *Package Goods* are stenciled under a tar-paper overhang. The four boys went into one of these bars.

They drank. They must have reassured each other in the stiff, terse way of boys and men. You can imagine Hood drunk with fascination about what had happened but careful not to show weak-seeming curiosity.

At some point Loco and Woo left. Perhaps they went to Woo's place where the pants and phone were supposedly later seen. They were just the instruments of murder, which were now put away. For Hood the evening wasn't over.

If Hood arrived at the bar at five thirty or six, he had a long time to get grimly and pleasantly dizzy about the murder he'd ordered. Several others joined him and McClean. Michael Fitzgerald is the only one who's been identified. The next time we hear about the group it's around two thirty a.m. Hood, McClean, and Fitzgerald (plus the one or two unknowns) drove to Baltimore and South Streets. They parked two cars, Hood's and an old red Saturn of Fitzgerald's, in a parking garage on the northeast corner of the intersection.

This is the heart of downtown Baltimore. The '80s Chamber of Commerce building stands across Baltimore Street from the parking garage. City Hall is a block north and east. From here South Street runs a couple of blocks into the Inner Harbor and the berth of the museum ship sloop-of-war USS *Constellation*.

Catercorner to the parking garage is the handsome American Building, the old home of the long-defunct *Baltimore American* newspaper. The building has an ornate cast-iron façade painted dark green, which now frames the windows of a twenty-four-hour 7-Eleven. The garish red and green 7-ELEVEN sign makes for a jarring contrast to the faded gilt of the Gothic black-letter *Baltimore American* above it.

At two thirty, the fluorescent-lit 7-Eleven must have been the brightest place around. The entrance is at the corner of the building, a vestibule with glass doors opening onto both South and Baltimore Streets. Three guys happened to be waiting near the South Street entrance: Jermaine Kelley, Brandon Sanders, and, just across the street, Christopher Webster. They were waiting on Howard and Davon Horton, who were picking up a few things in the store. The kids were dressed a little ghetto— Gucci sunglasses, diamond studs—but they weren't gang members.

From the garage across the intersection comes a group of black guys, strung out like wolves. Hood, McClean, Fitzgerald, more. One of this group, unidentified except that he was wearing a white baseball cap, walks up to Webster. He lifts the front of his shirt to show he's carrying a handgun. He takes it out.

Brandon Sanders, who was nearest the 7-Eleven entrance, ducked inside and told Howard and Davon, "Guy got a gun on your cousin, man!"

Howard looked out the window and saw Webster leaning against the granite footing of the Chamber of Commerce building across the street. Some guy in a white hat was talking to him, but it didn't look like a robbery.

So Howard steps out to find out what's going on. As he does, he sees his cousin taking off his shoes (to prove he has no money hidden), and he sees the guy in the white cap slip the gun back into his "dip area," as they call it in Baltimore.

Before he can react, Michael Fitzgerald, one of the guys who'd joined Hood and McClean, grabs Howard's arms from behind. "Empty your pockets!"

Howard figured this guy had a gun as well, so he fished four or five dollars from his front left pocket. Fitzgerald meanwhile slipped a hand into Howard's right front pocket and took Davon's car keys (Howard had been driving his brother's car), before ordering him, "Push it down the street!"

All this happened so quickly, Jermaine Kelley was still standing there at a complete loss. Fitzgerald swung toward him and grabbed the Cincinnati Reds cap from his head. Curtis McClean approached and ordered Jermaine to take out his diamond earrings. "Gimme your wallet and glasses!" Fitzgerald added. And after Jermaine gave them everything, Fitzgerald shouted, "Get the fuck out of here!"

While this was happening, Davon slipped out of the 7-Eleven and hurried down South Street. Not fast enough. One of the attackers (unknown) demanded his watch. Davon refused.

Someone yelled, "Just shoot him! Just shoot him!" This could have been Hood's second fiat for murder that day, but nobody knows who did the yelling. In any case, the attacker dutifully shot Davon three times—chest, shoulder, hip. Each bullet went clean through him. (Davon lived, barely.)

The shooter ran down South Street. The rest of them backtracked to the parking garage, where it happened a plainclothes detective was working that night. A police car was also sitting two blocks east on Baltimore Street. It made a U-turn and got to the intersection in seconds. The plainclothes detective caught Fitzgerald by his car. After more police arrived and the garage had been sealed off, officers approached a Dodge Avenger with tinted windows. Both seats were laid out flat. Two people were hiding. On the passenger's side: McClean. A hollow point bullet fell from his pants when he responded to the order to get out. Lying flat in the driver's seat: Hood. What was on that motionless, serious boy's mind as he ended his career as a leader in a shabby robbery like this?

Something rare happened in this case. Despite the baby faces involved, despite the nice Randallstown families, this was an authentic gang murder. Loco and Woo were caught easily enough, but neither they nor anyone else would name names because of the gang connection. Detectives Gary Childs and Joseph Caskey (who ran the case from the beginning) simply didn't believe Loco and Woo's gay story at first. The detectives were probably too grown-up or too sophisticated to understand or remember the bizarre, boyish ideal of impeccable manliness. Indeed, the gangs frequently mystified them. Childs shook his head when he told me about a boy who admitted shooting somebody simply because "he was mugging me," Baltimore slang for staring at him.

Woo, with his shaggy dreads, his raggedy beard coming

to a point, with a heaviness around his hips that gave his thuggish appearance a trace of cowlike gentleness, eventually told his father everything—the gang, the order to kill. His father had no advice except a halting, automatic, and insufficient, "You gotta do the right thing."

If he cooperated with prosecutors, Woo would have to worry for the safety of his grandmother Bercille, his father, his entire family. He'd have to serve his time in protective custody. Out of genuine remorse, apparently, he finally did talk. He talked about the birthday party and the meeting at Mondawmin Mall and the order, mentioning a name detectives had never heard and would never have known: Hood, Timothy Rawlings Jr., a kid in jail in the city for some 7-Eleven robbery.

In an uncanny moment before Hood was sentenced to life without parole, he was permitted to review the "pre-sentencing report"—a private document full of victim impact statements and mitigating information about the defendant. Sitting at the defense table, the small, self-possessed boy bent forward studiously and turned the pages very slowly with a steady hand.

As I watched him, the question came to mind, *Is he really reading?* His lawyers whispered between themselves. The aristocratic, white-haired Judge Robert Dugan waited impassively. A court officer reminded people to keep their cell phones silent. This was mainly directed at the six gang members in the last row on Hood's side of the room. They're children, basically, slight of build and posturing in their seats with an impudence that looks as stylized as that in *West Side Story*. Yet these boys will kill.

Still, Hood turns the pages, keeping the whole courtroom waiting without any sign of self-consciousness. He

hasn't been sentenced yet, but he must know what's coming. Two teachers, a ponytailed white guy and an African
American woman, guide their black students—mostly girls
in white sweaters—into the courtroom. The students and
their teachers all wear an uplifting button that reads: *Live Your
Dreams*. But as Hood continues turning the pages, reading his
own life, the teachers whisper and the students are—a little
disruptively—led out again. Hood keeps turning the pages.

His mother Tereia, the corrections officer, will heave
herself to her feet and say her son isn't the monster he's
been painted to be. "But I want to apologize for my son's
alleged actions." She'll turn to address the Parrishes directly with lawyer-tutored formality.

Michelle Parrish will also go forward to speak from
the prosecution table. She'll start uncertainly, then be-
rate Hood like any mother. During her furious remarks,
the gang members will suddenly be led from the room by
Childs and Caskey. The detectives will explain to me later
that the kids were making intimidating hand signals.

For now, Hood turns the pages, delaying his sentencing and seemingly in complete mastery of time itself.

Michelle Parrish saved her greatest venom for Loco, Steven
Hollis, the best friend. His sentencing came several weeks
later. The prosecutor phoned for an extra court officer in
case gang members showed up again, but Loco's side of
the courtroom was entirely filled by his somber relatives
led by his father, a slight man in an orange shirt and a boxy
pale-green suit.

The Parrishes, with one set of grandparents, sat behind
a couple of reporters on the prosecution side. Though Michelle had sobbed and Steven Sr. had toyed obsessively

with his BlackBerry before Woo's sentencing (Juan Flythe, who'd cooperated) and before Hood's (Timothy Rawlings Jr.), this morning the Parrishes appeared more relaxed. It was their third time, after all. Everybody was waiting for Judge Dugan and the prisoner.

A minor flutter arose among the Parrish family when Steven Sr. found he'd misplaced his free-parking ticket. As he searched his jacket pockets, laughing softly at his own forgetfulness, one of the grandparents leaned in and joked, "This happens when you get to be the over-the-hill kind." More whispered chuckles all around.

Michelle's attention crossed the aisle only once. She put her arms on the back of the bench in front of her. She leaned forward and cocked her head pointedly at the crowd of Hollises on the other side of the room. Through her stylish narrow glasses, she gave them a good long look, which none returned.

When it came her time to speak, Michelle tugged at her yellow sweater and strode forward, confident-seeming. She was wearing slacks for the first time. "I need to make sure my son . . ." And she immediately broke down. She wept. After gathering herself, she spoke faster, and her voice quickly rose almost to a shout. "I can't believe how somebody's *best friend* could kill them! To have someone you claimed to *love* as a brother, someone you *knew* was not gay . . . *You knew he was not!*" Many of the Hollises stifled sobs. "That's not love. That's hate. And no amount of sorrys can make it better." She turned to Judge Dugan: "I do not want him out!" And back to Loco: "I want every time you see me to remember that's why you're in there, because of what you did! I will never forgive you! You have *ruined* my life!"

Steven Hollis Sr. spoke on behalf of his son. He had

a halting, preacherly eloquence. He clasped his hands together when he faced his old friends. "Michelle, I am so sorry. Steven was my son. Steven *is* my son. Don't let that hatred sit in your heart. If I could take it back I would. I warned him about hanging out with a gang . . ."

Mr. Hollis shifted his weight. In his effort to remain poised, he seemed to lose track of his plea for a moment. "This is his family." He gestured toward the Hollises. "And *this* is his family." Shyly, he extended his cupped hands toward the Parrishes. He recalled Thanksgivings and family gatherings they'd all shared. Soft-spoken, he wondered aloud, "If there was *any* way to . . ." Terribly diminished after his speech, holding onto a bare shred of formality, he finished, "It's all such a waste."

Loco had none of his father's gift for speaking. When he finally stood and turned, he looked more confused than ever under his frightening frown. He was no longer the 190-pound football player he used to be. In prison he'd been gradually losing weight, ten, thirty, fifty pounds. He was gaunt now. He was being eaten up. I thought of the way a wasp larva devours its host from the inside with instinctive care to keep the meal alive till the last possible moment.

Loco pressed the tips of wonderfully long, slender fingers on the defense table. They bent backward. In a voice as soft as his father's but gruffer, clumsier, he said, "I just want to make my apologies to Ms. Michelle. I hope that one day you can forgive me . . . Steven is gone, but he's still my best friend."

As if this were a Baptist church, the Parrish grandparents couldn't repress a muted response. "Hm-*mm*, hm-*mm*," they disagreed. With hushed precision they said, "No, he is not."

7
GANGS AND LONERS

Violence by groups, no matter how grisly or perverse, feels different to the participants. Soldiers and executioners aren't murderers. They're respectable participants in the state monopoly on violence— at least they're supposed to be. In reality, executioners have always been regarded with unease, and soldiers returning from a war, especially in our ultrapeaceable society, are subject to almost unbearable alienation.

If things feel ambiguous to individuals when the state has an accepted right to its monopoly on violence, they become even more desperate psychologically under a criminal regime. The delusions of ex-Nazis and ex–Khmer Rouge are well-known and grotesque.

Most group violence takes place at a much smaller scale than the state. Though "gay panic" crimes are usually one-on-one, like Jonathan Schmitz and Scott Amedure, it's interesting that Matthew Shepard, Steve Domer, Billy Jack Gaither, and Gary Matson and Winfield Mowder were all killed by pairs of murderers. Some kind of minimal group sensibility was in play. Two may be the most dangerous number, but killings by larger groups and mobs occur as well. The gay man Michael Sandy was escaping four attackers when he was hit by a car and killed in Brooklyn in 2006.

When we talk about gang violence, though, we mean

something other than just a larger number of people were involved. As in Parrish's case (and he was actually killed by a pair, as well), there can be the simulacrum of a trial. The participants engage in a pretense of civilized behavior. They're conscious of communal honor. A decision is made, an order is given. There's at least a sham of "state" authority.

That authority is part of the attraction of gangs, and it may be the reason that gang members sometimes seem more recoverable than other criminals. Maybe they are. Maybe all it takes is growing up to reorient loyalty or to learn compassion. Hollis and Flythe (Loco and Woo) were pretty good kids, and who knows how they would have turned out if they'd been able to resist the pointless murder of a friend?

That's not to say gangs don't harbor psychopaths. But the relative "normality" of some of the participants and the sense of criminal justification gangs offer make their values paradoxically more terrifying to outsiders than those of an ordinary killer. They have real power. Probably the most famous gang of all is the Sicilian Mafia, a criminal state-within-a-state for much of its existence. Mafia values, including an obsession with honor, "Family Over Everything," and a particular loathing for homosexuality, are stamped all over this book, though it's unlikely anyone I've written about knows much about the actual organization.

It's fitting to mention the case of Leonardo Vitale. In Italian, what we call a "Mafia turncoat" is a *pentito*. Whatever you call them, they're usually people trying to save their own skin. But in Vitale's case (as with Juan Flythe), actual repentance was involved. He showed up at a Palermo police station in 1973 and spontaneously announced that he was a Mafia captain (*capodecino*) undergoing a spiritual crisis. He confessed to a kidnapping and two murders and described as much of the Mafia organization as he was privy to. He'd been raised by his uncle, who became his *capo* and who introduced him to murder gently by ordering him to kill a horse, first, then a man. (Exactly the old story of the knight inuring his son to slaughter.)

Because his behavior after turning himself in was so erratic, Vitale was deemed *seminfermità mentale*, and no one believed most of what he said. In 1977, after a trial based on his confessions, twenty-six defendants were released for lack of evidence. Only Vitale and his uncle went to prison. Vitale spent most of his incarceration in a mental institution. After his release in '84, everything he'd said was confirmed by a much higher-ranking *pentito*. A few months later, in December of '84, coming out of Mass with his mother and sister, Vitale was shot twice in the head. The famous Mafia prosecutor Giovanni Falcone, who was assassinated himself in '92, wrote an article called "The Importance of Leonardo Vitale," and the case of the "crazy" mafioso, the first *pentito*, the one no one believed, has been made into a book and movie in Italy.

Falcone, and Italians in general, either never mention or they downplay one of the most intriguing aspects of the Vitale story. Life within a criminal regime, or a shadow regime in this case, might drive anyone mad, but Vitale had his own reasons both for joining and for leaving the Mafia. The driving force throughout his life was an unrelenting crisis of masculinity. *"Credevo di essere un pederasta e me lo sono portato sempre dietro questo pensiero."* [I thought I was a fag and I always carried that thought around inside me.] He became a mafioso *"per protestare contro la mia natura, perché Dio me aveva creato quei complessi . . . Una protesta contro Dio, per il complesso di non essere uomo*" [to protest against my nature, because God had given me this obsession . . . It was a protest against God for my obsession about not being a man]. Vitale's return to faith, his confession, was probably as much an attempt to escape homosexuality as the Mafia. Tragically for him, whether as mafioso or *pederasta*, there was no way to escape a life of "crime."[9]

Vitale's sense of isolation must have been intense, both within the Mafia and in Sicilian society at large, exactly the solitude gang life is supposed to correct. Like the straight boy Juan Flythe in Baltimore, Vitale did finally try to live up to his own peculiar notion of goodness, though he had to do it alone. Some people are more comfortable going solo, and they may not be reaching for goodness at all but *embracing* a Nazi- or Mafia-like inversion of morality on their own. No gang needed. The last case in this volume is about someone like this.

There's a chance this killer was at least vaguely aware of the whole concept of gay panic. He may have counted on it for safety when, for much more obscure reasons, he killed. He may have had an instinct that the public would despise his victim, exactly as it turned out many people did, and he may even have been canny about his status as a "juvenile" or about possessing what I earlier called "cuteness." Whether such unnerving and dark confidence was real—I fear it was—this killer was still heartbreakingly young.

---

9. I owe those quotations and much of Vitale's story to John Dickie's history, *Cosa Nostra* (Palgrave McMillan, 2004). The translations are mine.

8
WEBER AND KATEHIS, 2009

I. *Boy, Man*

On March 22, 2009, a Sunday, the actual drama—murder, flight, capture—was almost over. But the news was coming out faster and faster, like the spokes of a wheel going blurry, then oddly static: there was too much information to process. Everyone involved, down to the accused murderer's family cat Fluffy, had a presence on the Internet. MySpace, Craigslist, YouTube, twistedsiblings.com, georgeweber.net, ibeatyou.com, XTube, vampirefreaks.com.

Murders are mostly local news. Like all great international cities, New York also has a local side, a sort of urban private life that isn't necessarily part of its public image. For instance, when outsiders hate or adore "New York," the boroughs other than Manhattan often don't figure in their thoughts. This was a local story, a Brooklyn and Queens story. Even the Manhattan part of it—the media-insidery sifting through all that titillating online "evidence"—was somehow local, an example of the cozy Manhattan compulsion to act more dreadful than you think you really are, to signal that you're wise to the world.

A body was found in the parlor-floor apartment of a brownstone in the Carroll Gardens neighborhood of Brooklyn, right around the corner from the 76th Precinct house. This wasn't the fanciest section of rapidly gentrifying Carroll Gardens; the buildings on this stretch of Henry Street weren't all fussily restored. The area looked a lot like neighborly New York of a long time ago. Indeed, many old-timers still lived there, and newcomers had adopted their habit of weekend stoop sales. You got a few dollars and unloaded junk like LPs, that ironic Elvis plate, or a birdcage spray-painted gold. But the March Sunday when the body was found was too early in the season for the sales to start. It was cool. The street was empty. Stubborn brown leaves from the previous fall hung on the ends of twigs.

Coworkers worried about the victim when he missed a Saturday shift. They called the police. Cops walked around the corner from the 76th Precinct house to the Henry Street building for the first time just after midnight. Nothing seemed amiss. After more anxious calls, they came back at eight thirty Sunday morning. This time a neighbor mentioned hearing the water running in the parlor-floor apartment. The water had been running for days. Something was wrong.

For the rest of the day it was cop cars, news vans, the medical examiner's truck, yellow tape, idling videographers. A man in a white jumpsuit appeared at the front door and ushered out two others in ME windbreakers, who maneuvered gingerly down the stoop carrying a body in a thick black vinyl bag lashed to a spine board.

Because it was the weekend, the story began the old-fashioned way: information was gathered by reporters who called up police press officers and wrote squibs for newspapers and wire services. The local TV stations made a chopped salad of old images of the victim, of the black bag coming down the stairs, of God-I-can't-believe-it interviews with neighbors. As those images shuffled in the background of one broadcast, a plummy voice-over droned the usual platitudes: "A man who lived for the news, who, with his tragic death, is now making the news . . ." Because, ironically, the victim had been a reporter too. The *Daily News* and the *New York Post* love murders. They dove in. But even the *New York Times* put the story on page eighteen of its Sunday "Region" section. The local New York edition only, but still.

The victim, it turned out, was well-known locally. He had that hale-fellow-well-met retail fame that prompts the owners of your favorite bars and restaurants to ask if they can hang your picture on the wall. (*Best Lasagna in New York!*) He was an ABC Radio newsman, George Weber. He even had a jaunty trademark, *George Weber, the news guy.* So, fairly or not, the news was already a little newsworthier than your average murder.

Mainstream reporters got the hard information efficiently. Weber was forty-seven (forty-eight if he'd lived until Monday, his birthday). He'd worked for about twelve years on various shows at the big New York affiliate, WABC NewsTalkRadio 77. He'd done the first two hours of *Curtis and Kuby in the Morning* as all but an equal partner. But that popular program, run by Curtis Sliwa (founder of the Guardian Angels in another lifetime) and attorney Ron Kuby, ended when the affiliate picked up Don Imus's *Imus in the Morning.*

Weber stayed on. He helped Michael Bloomberg on the mayor's Friday show. But he'd finally, and just recently, lost his job to cost-cutting. He found a little work at the affiliate's national network, WABC.

No longer a guy with a regular job, he was now a benefitless "freelance anchor." His news show was still picked up by owner-operated stations like 1010 WINS in New York. It was a typical "great recession" job story. He wrote about it—no sour grapes, of course—on a blog his friend and ex-producer Frank Morano encouraged him to start, georgeweber.net. "Hey, it's George Weber, the news guy . . ."

With so many media-savvy types surrounding Weber, it was simple work for reporters to get eulogistic quotes to plug into their stories. To a network vice president, Weber was "a consummate journalist." Ron Kuby spoke easily and eloquently about his ex-colleague to Tim Fleischer of ABC TV. Even the mayor issued a statement: "George called news events as he saw them with little regard to party politics or ideology."

On Monday, the police fanned out around the Henry Street brownstone. But the end came quickly. By Tuesday, with his own father's agonized participation, a suspect was captured (in Middletown, New York, about halfway to the Catskills).

When the suspect was driven back to the 76th Precinct from Middletown, he was apparently talking pretty freely. A Brooklyn assistant DA, Marc Fliedner, showed up at the precinct house to discuss charges. He spoke to the father. He interviewed the suspect on video. The city's police commissioner himself, Ray Kelly, gave a press conference describing in appropriately staid terms what sounded a lot like a gay hookup gone awry or even a hustler murdering his john. Apparently, the suspect had confessed.

Details started coming out that hinted at a salacious underside to Weber's eulogies. It had already been reported that he was stabbed anywhere from ten to fifty times, including defensive wounds to his hands. A witness had seen a man on a cell phone pacing in front of the Henry Street brownstone on Friday night. A neighbor had later heard a thump.

Now reports came out that the victim's legs, or both his hands and legs, had been bound with duct tape. An informant mentioned rough sex. There was no evidence of forced entry, so the victim knew his killer or at least opened the door for him. Word got out that drugs and alcohol were involved. Erotic snapshots were found in the apartment.

TV cameras were trained on the '60s modernist 76th Precinct building when the Middletown captive was led out. A young, thuggishly handsome man, shaved head, olive skin, handcuffed, he wore a teenager's, or criminal's, default expression of scorn. He looked at the cameras with black-eyed indifference. His upper lip was swollen, injured during the capture in Middletown. His black sweatshirt and khakis were oversized, though not in the fashionably baggy way. In fact, the police had given him these clothes. They kept as evidence what he'd been wearing when caught.

The kid was John Katehis (the middle syllable is stressed and rhymes with "say"), and, though he looked older, he was only sixteen, a minor.[10] *SIXTEEN! ROUGH SEX! MURDER! FAMOUS NEWSMAN!* Even the dourest observer must have felt a shiver of tabloid fascination.

The media and gossip website Gawker, an aggregator and commenter on the news, had already noted Weber's murder over the weekend. The site, which is famous for half-put-on/half-real Manhattan dreadfulness, has a keen moralistic streak invisible to many of its readers and, es-

---

10. An important detail: though it's not widely known, a sixteen-year-old in New York is a minor sexually but not criminally. Katehis was treated as an adult from start to finish.

pecially, to the targets of its scorn. Hamilton Nolan wrote a rueful post imagining the *Daily News*' description of the suspect as a male "companion" (his ironic quotes) and expected the *Post* to up the ante to "Sex Slay" in the title of a Tuesday article. "Not what . . . you would want your legacy to be immediately after your untimely death," he noted.

Tawdry or not, Nolan pursued the story with the you-decide completism of modern Internet journalism. He found Katehis's eerie MySpace page and countless photos of the accused killer posing with items from his very scary collection of knives. Nolan posted everything on Gawker, including links to Katehis's childish YouTube videos of himself: the boy giggles helplessly while listening to the crank phone calls he made for his site JSKCranks. In another he boasts with tough-guy profanity about a seventy-five-dollar bottle of "fucking" Absinthe he just bought, kisses it, and concludes, "Now I'm gonna go try me some of this fucking shit."

Nolan even put up a link to the diciest item Katehis had online. As "greekjohn92," Katehis had posted on XTube a forty-six-second video of himself with the descriptive title, "Wanking my semi-soft uncut cock." From a steep overhead angle, against a background of dun carpet, the faceless video shows an olive hand doing exactly what the title says to a darker olive penis. "Semi-soft" may betray a touch of cautious underselling from an otherwise cocky boy, but the video is just what you'd expect from a kid showing off his junk. A Gawker commenter pointed out that since everyone now knew greekjohn92 was sixteen instead of eighteen (as his XTube profile claimed), maybe it was best to leave the link alone for legal reasons.[11] Gawker removed it.

---

11. Katehis's XTube account was set up on December 16, 2006, and he hadn't signed in for a year before the murder, so he was actually only fifteen in the video.

What kind of a sixteen-year-old was this? Would his MySpace self-portrait really be so eerie except in retrospect?

My name is John, I am sixteen years of age and live in Queens, New York. I enjoy long conversations, drinking, bike riding, hanging out, roof hopping, hanging off trains, any type of Parkour exercise, Extreme Violence (chaos, Anarchy, ect..) Video Games, Violent Movies and listening to my ipod. I am a very easy person to talk to. I like to do crazy and wild things. im like an adrenaline junkie, I'm always looking for a big thrill, I'm a big risk taker and like to live life on the edge.I am an Extremist, an Anarchist,and a Sadomasochist. As long as you show respect for me i will show respect for you, if you disrespect me, then i will fucking break your neck. To learn more about me just send me a message or catch me on aim, my screen name is johnkatehis92, my yahoo is greeksatan92@ yahoo.com, johnkatehis92@yahoo.com and my msn is greek-john92@hotmail.com. You can ask me any kind of questions, I am always happy to chat with a new person. Oh and be sure to check out my crank call videos at youtube.com/JSKCranks, and see if u can beat any of my challenges or beat my scores at challenges, at ibeatyou.com my screen name is crazyjohn92.
[sic throughout]

The "92" that keeps showing up refers to his birth date, June 26, 1992.

It's simple to identify the quotes that caught journalists' attention. Here was a kid who would break your neck if you dissed him. But maybe it wasn't as scary as that. XTube has convenient switches to indicate your own sex and the sex of the person you're interested in. Katehis was signed up as an eighteen-year-old male interested in women. His hobbies were buying swords, playing video games, fighting, and sex. His self-presentation, including flaunting his penis, makes him look like a precocious and arrogant fifteen-year-old trying to intrigue dream-babes. Since he hadn't logged on for a year, the babes must not have been beating down his door.

Based on his confessions, the story came out that Katehis had responded to Weber's "Adult Gigs" post on Craigslist. That could have been a one-time thing, an easy sixty bucks. What really seemed strange was Weber's fetish. The title of his post was "Smotherme." He liked to be smothered, and that's what he'd hired this risk-taking kid to do.

Soon this material was all over news sites, and Internet commenters started to weigh in. Katehis had to be at least bi. He was gay and obviously couldn't deal with it. No! Weber was the criminal! A forty-seven-year-old pedophile having sex with a kid. He deserved it. Katehis just went over on a lark and freaked out. But look at those pictures of him with his machetes! What about his parents? Anybody who would do that is obviously a demented fag. Good riddance to both of them. Some, who claimed to know Katehis or to be fellow students of his, said, "He was quiet," "He's not a tough guy," "It's so weird."

The anonymous commentariat debated pedophilia vs. ephebophilia and whether smothering counted as sex, because real sex had to cost more than sixty dollars, and what was the ultimate responsibility of a sixteen-year-old, anyway—all this time joking with the Internet's usual clever, postprivate savagery—and the aggregate judgment turned against Katehis. There were a few firebrands like "Damian Hospital" who railed against Weber the pedophile in a long series of posts, and shouted a rhetorical

"FREE JOHN KATEHIS!" into the hush of the web. In his opinion, "that sick bastard" Weber's reputation was being protected by bigwig media friends.

To most people, Katehis seemed troubled and troubling. He went to a special school in Westchester. Online he claimed to be a satanist. As "John Psychedelic," he put up a page on twistedsiblings.com (a Goth-oriented social site linked to but not affiliated with MySpace) that included a self-description more or less identical to the MySpace one. But instead of breaking necks, he warns, "I don't take shit from anybody, so if your [sic] looking for problems, fuck off!" And between "anarchist" and "sadomasochist" he adds that he's a "LaVeyan satanist."

John Psychedelic's twistedsiblings page is a red and black symphony of pentagrams, a horned devil, and a large background photo of Anton LaVey. There's an image of a lapel button with the slogan, *I HATE christians*.

Katehis's satanism turns up everywhere. In scores of online pictures Katehis is almost always doing one of three things: brandishing a knife, giving the camera the finger, or, very frequently, making the devil's horns sign with his index and fifth fingers. He has a large tattoo of a pentagram on his right shoulder with 6-6-6 between the star's upper points and *Diablo* in gothic letters below. He often appears wearing a silver pentagram around his neck and another on the middle finger of his right hand. His T-shirts (always black) advertise ghoulish third-wave heavy metal bands like Cannibal Corpse, Lamb of God, the Black Dahlia Murder.

But how seriously can you take a sixteen-year-old's infatuation with satanism? Even with the tattoo. Heavy metal music and antisocial anger are part of the classic teenage bag of tricks. Furthermore, Katehis specifies *LaVeyan* satanism.

Though books on satanism were found at his family home (Katehis's father later tells me they were his own), it's unlikely Katehis could have read deeply about an occult practice that has hardly any depth to begin with. LaVeyan satanism isn't what it sounds like. A 1960s Hollywood invention of Anton LaVey, it began as more of a Playboy Mansion party than a coven. It denies the existence of God and Satan both. Despite its original, spooky *mise-en-scène*, LaVeyan satanism's tenets are actually rather humane. There's a blanket, hedonistic replacement of indulgence for abstinence, but adherents are expected to behave pretty well. Still, vengeance is prescribed over turning the other cheek. And if someone in your home annoys you, you're meant to treat them cruelly and without mercy. Maybe this is what Katehis was getting at when he talked about breaking necks.

The satanic details are beside the point. If Katehis had been going to Exeter, say, instead of a school for troubled kids in Westchester, he might well have fixated on Nietzsche. Katehis's "LaVeyan satanism" is the masculine ideal of perfect self-reliance. Many boys are drawn to that fantasy. For them, the simplistic seems stronger than kryptonite. When they read, "Anything that doesn't kill me makes me stronger," they feel like they've been struck by intellectual lightning. How serious could this boy be?

At the same time, George Weber now appeared before the public completely exposed. You just couldn't get more naked. He would have hated it. He would have raged or died of shame. First off, he didn't think of himself as gay. Besides harboring a different set of desires, he had the waning white-picket-fence hopes that often afflict very cheerful, very public personalities. Friends, family, *no one*, knew about his secret fetish except the hustlers he hired. One of them remembers spotting George with a crowd of bar friends in Brooklyn. They exchanged a glance of fond but forlorn knowingness straight out of the 1950s. The hustler, ex- by that time, says he understood not to say hello.

A blue-collar social philosopher before bouncing around the country for his radio career, Weber had grown up outside of Philadelphia. His parents still lived there, as did a sister with a perfect, straight-arrow husband. Weber might as well have been South Boston Irish, though. The blarney, the relentless good cheer, the ethics veering between maudlin and vengeful, the pretty serious alcoholism. He had a hard drinker's gut and a hard drinker's bloated face, pillowy along the jawline. He had wispy hair and bad skin, pasty and prone to flush. He looked older than he was.

Apart from the bar friends and the media friends and the neighbors, Weber's social world revolved around his beloved dachshund Noodles and, for more articulate intimacy (and sex), hustlers. They talked to him. And he talked to them. It was friendly. He explained to one that the smothering thing started when he was a kid. An older boy had wrestled him to the ground and put his hands over his mouth. Somehow Weber remembered liking it—the scare, the contact eroticism. For an irrepressible talker like him, a story was a much better explanation than anything as dryly descriptive as "autoerotic asphyxiation."

In any case, smothering worked for him. One guy who answered his "Smotherme" ad on Craigslist explained that Weber never even took his clothes off. He would lie supine on the bed, maybe gripping the thin steel bars of the headboard. The hustler said all he had to do was straddle him, clamp down on Weber's mouth and nose, and Weber, staring at his own reflection in a cheval glass tipped over the bed, would eventually come. Meanwhile, the hustler gazed at a black-and-white art photograph of a movie-house marquee hanging on the wall over the bed. If he got bored, he confessed, he might press down a little to make George come faster. But that was it. It was hardly sex at all.

Fetishes are by definition unusual, but this one was particularly eerie. After all, it was flirting with death. People shied from imagining it. At one point, the no-nonsense trial judge Neil Firetog couldn't keep himself from calling it "this smothering garbage." The hustler remembers the movie marquee photo so well because he was avoiding looking down at George's face. The broken capillaries disappeared in an all-over redness, purpleness, and somehow the eyelids gaped slightly as if air or blood were straining at ducts around the eyeballs. One time, smothering George from behind for a change, he says George lost consciousness, becoming dead weight as a few tablespoons of vomit slipped from his mouth. Thinking he'd killed him, knowing he could have, the hustler refused to see George ever again.

George went on, though. He got into light bondage. Sometimes he was short of cash. Perhaps, every time he had sex, he felt a self-disgust as elaborate, as ceremonial, as his sexual practices had become. But outwardly he was a sweetheart, loved by neighbors, coworkers.

His secret hustler family liked him too. In fact, the hustlers worried about his getting into trouble. All was innocent enough while George sat watching wrestling on TV until he was aroused, but then he'd lead any stranger into the bedroom where everything was set up. One of his regulars, a young man who bore a striking resemblance to John Katehis, said he talked with friends about the danger George ran of meeting the wrong guy.

Mostly George was alone. He'd drink rum-and-cokes from the moment he came home, or wander down to Angry Wade's, a faux-old sawdusty red stucco tavern on Smith Street with a roaring animal head on a shield over the door and football on the wide-screen TVs.

Even after Noodles suddenly died, George planned his second annual Noodlepalooza party. He cadged refrigerator space for beer from a neighbor, throwing out jovially, "Oh, and you can come too!" The marquee guests at the first Noodlepalooza had been Joe Franklin and Bernie Goetz (a weird New York personality locally famous since his 1984 vigilante subway shooting spree). This time George had a crowd of sixty and an a cappella doo-wop group. He wrote about it on georgeweber.net.

On Friday, March 20, the day before he was killed, George uploaded a photograph of his thick ankle and lower leg to his blog. The hairless white skin was covered with red spots. In the accompanying post he wrote: "Many of you know I have had two bouts with bedbugs in my over ten years at this location in Carroll Gardens, so my radar is always on when it comes to the blood sucking bastards that made my life hell." He explains that he's gotten rid of them thanks to a good exterminator and comments on a political aspect of New York City's bedbug hysteria, then in full swing. "I predict, thousands of additional residents will be infested with bedbugs by the time this 'advisory board' reports back to the mayor with it's [sic] recommendations. Then, what? How much longer will it then take to

actually carry out the panel's advice? 2010? 2011? Too long!"
After posting that *cri de coeur*, maybe he glanced at his e-
mail from the day before. "From: Satan Katehis ‹greeksa-
tan92@yahoo.com› To: smother boy ‹handsmothered@hot-
mail.com› Hey dude its me John. I changed my number. my
new number is 347 634 0105."

II. *John's Version*

After he was tackled in Middletown, John told police his
name was Nick Smith. The playacting didn't last long.
While his father Spiro, who'd come along as part of a ruse,
was hustled back to Brooklyn in another car, John was
rear-handcuffed and put in a police department Chevy Impala. A Detective Yarrow drove. A second detective sat in
the front passenger seat. In back, next to John, sat a third
detective, James Normile, a trim gray-haired man with a
slight jowliness and the wide-open eyes and flat-footedness
of a TV second banana.

As Normile tells it, he explained to his prisoner that it
was going to be a long drive and that John could ask for a
bathroom stop if necessary. John began to relax. He said
he was sixteen. This was apparently his first truth. Maybe
he believed it would make a difference in the long run.
When asked what he wanted to be called, he told Normile
his real name was John. And he said he'd killed Weber by
accident, because the man had pulled a knife, and . . . At
this point, Normile says, he told John they could get into
the story back at the 76th Precinct (Miranda and all that).
So the exchange turned to small talk.

John may have been a little disconcerted to find the
detectives so unvengeful. Asked if Middletown was quiet,
he told the older men about the area's demographics. A lot

of Mexicans lived there. When a marked law-enforcement vehicle appeared on the highway next to them, he noted their own car was going over the speed limit and wondered jokingly if the Impala could make a getaway if this turned into "hot pursuit." By the end of the trip he was laughing now and then. He was still handcuffed.

Since the capture had occurred at about ten forty-five p.m., they didn't make it to the Brooklyn precinct house until one. Normile interviewed John with a colleague, and by two forty-five they had a written statement. Normile wrote it out himself in block print. A stitched-up injury had completely immobilized John's right forefinger, so he had trouble writing. Even so, before the interview, Normile was careful to get John to sign a simple form stating that he understood his Miranda rights. "Do you understand?" the form asked six times after spelling out each right. "Yes" was circled six times and John managed his initials "JSK" next to every one. After he finished writing the statement, Normile asked John to read and sign it as well. Did the kid want any changes made first? John asked only that "accidentally" be inserted before ". . . stabbing him in the neck."

Meanwhile, an assistant DA had shown up at the 76th Precinct. Marc Fliedner is a small man with an easy political glibness and the taste in blue suits and red ties to go with it. On this occasion he dressed down. He interviewed John on video at four twenty-three in the morning with Normile in the room.

III. The DVD

The DVD opens with a shot of what looks like an old movie clapper. A hand appears and writes in black marker,

"0423," the time. The hand then moves to the space for the name of the interviewee, "Jonathan Katehis," and crosses out "Jonathan," replacing it with "John." The camera pans to show who's in the room. After that, it's one long, unflinching shot of John.

The kid has the slightly ashen look the olive-skinned get when overtired or stressed. His buzz-cut hair and eyes have their usual obsidian gleam. But he's animated. He frequently swivels back and forth or shifts the entire chair on its wheels. His forearms only rarely come to rest on a yellow tabletop. Behind him are what look like closed metal shutters, a grated radiator, and over one shoulder, the clapper-like card is stuck to a wall now. On the table are the black mic and a half-eaten donut on a blue-rimmed plate.

John is wearing a black bomber jacket over a T-shirt. He speaks with a trace of the tough guy's *d'ese*-and-*d'ose* outer-borough accent. Sometimes his voice rises in a staccato *ha-ha-ha* of nervous laughter. A man-among-men baritone returns abruptly. Throughout the interview he has a blustery confiding tone, as if he believes that, through sheer energy, he can make his listeners understand what it was like to be in his shoes.

While his right hand, the injured one with an immobile, slightly curving forefinger, is surprisingly kinetic, his left hand is even busier. Whenever he isn't making explanatory gestures or stroking the side of his nose, which he does a couple of times (a tic reputed to betray liars), John uses his left hand constantly to dust donut crumbs from himself. He does this with an unexpected, aristocratic finickiness. He doesn't often pick up a piece of the broken donut. He takes a bite two or three times at most. But his elegant fingers twiddle endlessly over the plate as if his hand were an infinite source of crumbs or stickiness.

In response to Fliedner's questioning (on the DVD the ADA comes across as abundantly patient and relaxed yet serious), John tells the story, some details of which were soon to leak.

John says he sold a Sidekick and another smartphone on Craigslist and he was checking around the site and found a "smother thing" in the "Adult Gigs" section. He figured it would be an easy sixty dollars. He and George exchanged pictures. George's weren't explicit, just hands over his mouth and nose, and John thought he could do that. They had a back-and-forth about setting up a time, and John finally took the subway to Carroll Gardens on a Friday afternoon. He picked up a pack of M&Ms and a Stewart's root beer (probably at the Rite-Aid next to the subway entrance on Smith Street). He says he followed George's directions to 561 Henry Street, which was a straight shot past Carroll Park, down President Street.

In front of the Henry Street brownstone, John continues on the DVD, he phoned George. George came to the front door and let him in. John was still carrying his root beer, but he must have been about finished, because George offered him a Bud Light as soon as they got in the apartment. In an odd detail that must refer to Noodlepalooza 2, John says the older man joked that he had a lot of beer left over from a party. His friends had run through all the hard stuff. George was drinking something himself, but John doesn't know what. It was in a red plastic glass later found in the bedroom— maybe rum-and-Coke. After a minute of beer talk, George said, "Let me show you what's going on in the other room."

On the bed in the bedroom (here, John speaks to the ADA and detective with a buddylike expression of shared distaste) were mirrors, black duct tape, and rope and scissors. George explained how he like to be smothered, and John tried it, gingerly putting his hand over George's mouth and nose without pressing down.

After that delicate introduction to his fetish, George led John back into the living room. George had a chest he used as a coffee table. According to John, the inside of the chest was strewn with loose cocaine. On the DVD John tries to be helpful: "I assume it was cocaine. You guys have got to test it." George took some out and cut three lines for John but had none himself. "I was hyperjumpy after that. I don't take drugs. I'm—I got super paranoid." He says George explained that he wanted "the stuff you use to clean VCR tapes" sprayed on a sock and held to his mouth. (In the written statement he'd called this stuff "poppers.") "VCR tapes?" the ADA wonders. John lets out a high-pitched laugh, "VCR, yeah, I thought it was extinct."

George and John returned to the bedroom. They were both clothed. George got on the bed. John says he wrapped the duct tape around the man's ankles three or four times. Helpfully again, he explains that if police found any tape on his hand it must have been from when George was trying to get it off his ankles later, after the struggle. But George was on his stomach at this point. John says the older man turned over and pulled a knife from his pocket, probably just to show it off or something, but "I'm jumpy as shit from what I just told you." On the DVD he examines his dirty nails for a moment.

Fliedner asks, "Are you on the bed?" John shakes his

head and spits out a fleck of something before saying no. Then, in order to demonstrate how George must have pulled the knife from his right pocket after turning over, John briefly makes as if he's George lying on the bed. He says he (John) freaked out and grabbed for the knife.

Like someone patting a ball of dough into shape, he mimes their wrestling for the knife with his hands. Pressed, he says, "I'm leaning over the bed." He leans. "He's lying on his back." He leans back. He raises his voice a bit: "Both of our hands were on the knife. We were fussing over this knife." He was cut himself in the struggle. He holds up the injured finger.

More questions: "What were you talking about? Was there any conflict?"

In a striking flash of anger, John raises his voice: "NO! It was like I just told you. We were fussing over the knife and it slips and goes into his neck and he starts cursing and shit."

John is at once calm again. He returns to the scene. "I'm bleeping paranoid. Here I don't remember the sequence."

Fliedner asks whether John was carrying any knives himself. He mentions that John's own father said he usually carried two. But John had already explained in the written statement that he had no knife on him because he was coming straight from school where you weren't allowed to carry a knife. On tape, he repeats, "I just said I came from school." The preposterous idea of carrying knives to school causes him to erupt, "Ha-ha-ha!" with the same strained, high-pitched laughter as before.

Now, on the DVD, the wheels of John's chair squeak suddenly. He leans forward and grabs his right thigh. He's felt a shooting pain. Fliedner asks if he wants to stand up or stop. But John says the pain is "from the antibiotics or something."

Meanwhile, in court, while the DVD is being played, John's cheeks have turned distinctly red under his terra cotta complexion. No one enjoys seeing themselves "played back." John's father Spiro has scuttled from one side of the courtroom to the other to get a better view of the video. He can't stop sniffling, sobbing almost, as he watches.

The video interview continues. "It's all out of sequence," John says. "This dude's fucking stabbed and I'm bleeding the hell out of my hand . . ." He says he "ran around searching for shit." He took a bottle of whiskey and "chugged" some, but stopped because he wasn't sure if it might thin his blood and make the bleeding worse.

"I don't know how I did it so fast," he explains when asked why he went through George's collection of children's lunch boxes—twenty of them lined up atop the kitchen cabinets. He found "like just sippy cups" inside, "Ha-ha-ha!" Up on the countertop he started to feel dizzy. He ran water from the kitchen faucet over his deeply cut finger.

He went into the bathroom and tried to rinse the finger again but the water was too hot, so he took the lid off the toilet tank to soak his hand in cold water. He found some gauze bandages and tape in "the—like—the—" he makes an oddly elegant movement with his left hand and Fliedner supplies the word "mirror." "Yeah."

His clothes were bloody, so he took them off. He didn't want to get blood on his sneakers or on his Harley jacket. Mentioning this, his hands gesture toward his lapels. "That jacket?" Fliedner asks in a how-bout-that tone of voice. Yes. John was trying to keep blood off the very jacket he's wearing during the interview. He explains he sprayed himself with some Axe body spray he found in the bathroom and dressed in some of George's clothes. He wore one of George's leather jackets and carried the Harley jacket in his left hand.

"I'm tripping, I'm paranoid," he emphasizes repeatedly. He says he went back into the bedroom where George was still mumbling. He reached into George's pocket and took sixty dollars, "what he was going to pay me for this smothering garbage." (It's a different-sounding dismissive from when the judge picks the phrase up later.) As John reached into George's pocket his hand dragged the older man's pants down, and the body, or still-softly-vocalizing man, fell onto the floor.

"He still has his boxers on," John answers Fliedner's question with a little frown of propriety. He says he picked up the knife and took it with him, a flip-knife with a tiny knob on the three-inch blade so it could be opened with one hand. In the written statement he'd judged it a pretty good knife but added that he had a nicer one in his own collection. ("Yeah, I like my swords and knives," he admits defensively to Fliedner on the DVD.)

"I close the door behind me. That's something I do everywhere." At the foot of the brownstone's steps, he says, he turned right, then right again on President Street. "I dispose" of the knife by throwing it by a tree. "I was walking calmly. I was walking quickly."

Whatever John had used to bandage his finger wasn't holding. He'd severed a small artery, so blood pulsed out with every systole. He'd need stitches or a tourniquet to stop it. In the subway, he says, a "Hindu" couple swiped a MetroCard for him at the turnstile. He took the G train north, back toward Queens. He moved from car to car; his bleeding was attracting too much attention. Wherever he sat, his throbbing forefinger filled the shallow depression of the plastic subway seat next to him with blood. A stranger fished a fresh sock from his gym bag and handed it to him to stanch the flow.

In Long Island City, at Court House Square, John left the G line to switch to a eastbound 7 train. That would take him to 90th Street and Elmhurst Avenue, the stop closest to home. At Court House Square, an elevated station, an MTA functionary wasn't as helpful as the Hindu couple. He refused to buzz John through the emergency exit for two dollars. He sold him a single-ride MetroCard instead. John made it up to the platform, but by now he'd lost so much blood that another MTA worker promptly sat him down and called 911. An EMT later testified that his pulse was undetectable. He lost consciousness several times and was, in fact, near death. But he recovered quickly as soon as the injury was treated.

So why did he flee to Middletown after getting stitched up at the Cornell Medical Center? "I was reading all this shit about like twenty stab wounds and no mention of the coke, so it looks like he was killed in cold blood. I panicked." He says he spent a night in Penn Station before taking the train to Middletown where he had friends. He got a call from his father, who told him he'd finagled a ride upstate from somebody for fifty dollars and would bring three hundred dollars to John. "You know the rest." In Middletown, Spiro called John from a parked Ford Explorer with tinted windows. John approached. Even before the three detectives got out, he could see his father wasn't alone. He ran. There were four other cars, ten or twelve detectives in all.

IV. Discrepancies

On March 18, John posted an ad on Craigslist: "Iphone 3G 16gb Unlocked . . . Also comes with alot of games. $500. Call me at 347 612 6013. Anytime after 6pm. or reply to this message." A few minutes later he posted another ad offering to sell "my Sidekick 08 for 120 bucks, phone only." Apparently he needed money. Six hours earlier, giving Craigslist the same reply e-mail, greeksatan92@yahoo.com, he'd posted in the "Casual Encounters" category, "I Blow 4 Cash – m4m." Though John had to enter eighteen as his age for the system to take the ad, the body of his post read, "I am a 16 yo dude looking for quick cash, im bi, white, and uncut. but im only into oral play. will blow guy of any age. but only 4 cash."

Within fifteen minutes he got a reply from George Weber. He got other replies too. In his responses he presents himself as young and sexually savvy, but the details shimmer a bit uncertainly. "Hey dude, i would come over and jack off for you. is that all ur asking for? im in need of serious cash, im an uncut white male, 19 yo . . . lol u can even take pics or record if u want." "hey dude, im a 17yo white greek irish and italian dude, uncut 5inch dick, but I only like oral play . . ." In a message to one guy the next day, the day before the murder, John sounds almost plaintive: "Hey whats up dude? don't you wanna meet me and have some oral fun. do u have a car? im available today from 5pm . . ."

Only the exchange with George seems to have gone anywhere.

John: ok ok. cool. how much are you willing to offer. im avail-
    able everyday . . . i attached a few pics.
George: cool . . . thanks for getting back. i have a few guys who
    [do] this tie up/smothering thing on me and I usually do $60
    for 30-minutes. let me know if ur interest . . . oh and what
    r ur stats?
John: oh yea dude. im totally interested. what do you mean
    by stats????

George sends some smothering pictures to see if "Satan Katehis" is all right with it.

John: lol yea I saw the pics, pretty cool stuff. im aprox 150lbs,
    5foot 11inches.

They have some trouble setting up a time. At one point John teases the older man, "youve been a bad boy eh. lol . . ." First the meeting is set for Thursday, then Saturday, then Friday. The last message from John comes Thursday, the one in which he gives George a new phone number.

A couple of oddities stand out in these e-mails. Though he gets the sexual lingo down (as anyone could who'd spent a few minutes looking through ads of this kind), John doesn't know what his "stats" are, and he says his dick measures five inches, which sounds perfectly realistic but too honest for an experienced hustler. Unless John was *underplaying* his measurement, because he had a notion that submissiveness in dick size, age, and all the rest is a plus in attracting another man (an idea one could argue was curiously masculine, even straight, since gay men are more used to the paradoxes of sissified or boyish tops and hairy, big-dicked bottoms).

Furthermore, the photos John sent of himself don't look quite right for a hookup. He's fully dressed and doesn't appear particularly friendly. In one he leans back like a rock guitarist making double devil's horns with his hands by his thighs. In fact, the whole "I Blow 4 Cash" premise is a little odd, since guys like John, if they're straight and at all experienced, know they can get at least sixty bucks for just standing there while someone else blows *them*.

A slight aura of inexperience means nothing when it comes to the business of sex, of course. Everyone's a beginner at some point. But it raises two interesting, contradictory possibilities: maybe John was a little into the idea of sex with a man, or maybe he was trying to entice a victim based on an imaginary version of gay sexuality. Either way, he wasn't responding to George's ad as he later claimed. George was responding to his.

When he was found by EMTs at the 7 train station, John was in shock, sweating, pale, cool to the touch. The EMTs elevated his legs, raised his bandaged hand, and took him in a scoop stretcher to an ambulance where they gave him oxygen. He soon had a detectable radial pulse. The whole time he was being treated John couldn't stop worrying about a bag he'd been carrying. "I need my bag. Please don't forget my bag," Valerie Vera-Tudela recalls him saying over and over. He explained that he'd came from Coney Island where he'd cut his finger on a Snapple bottle. (Later he said something about juggling bottles.) He told her he'd had no drugs or alcohol. His pupils looked fine.

On the ride to the hospital, Valerie says, John's color

came back, and by the time they reached Cornell he was even laughing a bit and "flirting" with her. Routine toxicology testing on John's blood showed no traces of alcohol or cocaine.

As for the white powder found in George's chest and other places in the apartment, it tested negative for cocaine and opium alkaloids. Furthermore, a gas chromatography/mass spectrometry test showed no "extra peaks" that would indicate any other controlled substance or medicines like aspirin or acetaminophen.

No test was available to find out what the powder actually was, but two bottles of identical-seeming white NIC Pro-Organic insecticide dust were found in the apartment. Nic is a natural insecticide advertised to work against roaches, ants, bedbugs, carpenter ants, fire ants, flies, lice, mites, scorpions, termites, and ticks. Though never brought up in court, Nic's ingredients are listed clearly on its website: "Composition: Active Ingredient: Mint__1%, Rosemary__1%. Inert ingredient: Limestone__98%." If inhaled, the first aid recommendation is "move to a ventilated area."

A ring of black duct tape was found around one of George's wrists. It isn't plausible, as John casually suggested on the DVD, that this was a piece of tape George tried to get off his ankles. The duct tape around his ankles was still intact.

The ring of black tape around George's wrist was sticking to the skin on one side, loose on the other. The medical examiner reported it slipped off with ease. The loose side of the ring was badly stretched and twisted. It seems obvious that the tape originally bound both wrists and that George was able to free one of his hands during a struggle.

In a coup de théâtre, the prosecutor, Anna-Sigga Nicolazzi, began her summation by claiming John had admitted as much. She cued the DVD interview to the moment Fliedner asks John how George was holding the knife when the struggle began. John mimes George's starting position by bringing his wrists together and raising them to just under his chin. "He was like this . . ." The prosecutor paused the DVD at the image.

Thirty or forty crime scene photographs were introduced into evidence. Hundreds were taken. Tavis Watson of the 76th Precinct was what's called the "first officer," the first cop on the scene of a crime and the one responsible for securing the area. He was the one who came to Henry Street at eight thirty that Sunday morning.

George's door was locked, but Watson and his partner roused a neighbor in the ground-floor apartment and made their way to the backyard. At the top of a few steps, the door to George's parlor-floor apartment was unlocked. As soon as he entered, Watson says, he recognized the smell of a dead body.

In the bathroom the water in the tub was running onto a crumpled pair of black jeans. A bloody washcloth and a bloody gauze pad were on the edge of the bathtub. An oval rug on the floor was splattered with blood. There were also bloody spots and partial footprints all over the tiny hexagonal floor tiles. More gauze pads and their Johnson & Johnson paper wrappings were strewn on the rug along with a bloody towel.

The water was running in the sink, splashing and rocking a bottle of Axe body spray to and fro. The medicine cabinet was open. The top of the toilet tank had been taken off and placed on the toilet seat. The top of the tank was spattered with blood and greenish shaving foam. A broad ribbon of blood ran down the toilet's ceramic belly. Two black socks and a stray gauze pad were later found soaking in the open toilet tank. (One of George's hustler pals recalls his bathroom being filthy whenever he came over, but in the photos it looks as if it had been remodeled not long ago. The tub and fixtures are new. The tacky souvenir lighthouse, which the boy remembered as symbolic of George's loneliness, is gone.)

The kitchen was a mess. Ordinary stained wood cabinets, all agape, lined the walls above and below a counter cluttered with kitchen equipment. Paper bags and dishware, apparently from the ransacked cabinets, littered a narrow kitchen rug. (A closet in the short hall back to the bathroom also spilled its contents.)

A bottle of Dewar's scotch was on the floor. A DNA swab later confirmed this was the whiskey John had chugged. In the sink, inside a large cooking pot, were an empty can of Stewart's root beer and another of Bud Light. Twenty nostalgic lunch boxes lining the top of the cabinets were in disarray. Each had been methodically opened.

Though blood swabs were taken from many places in the kitchen, the room's true "bloodiness" only showed up after the surfaces were painted with leucocrystal violet and photographed under UV light. All over the wood floor, all over the white countertop, dense footprints of stockinged feet glowed in an eerie blue. You could all but see someone—someone with a spade-shaped big toe—shuffling along the counter opening lunch box after lunch box.

There were more signs of a ransacking in the living

room. The bedroom, too, was in complete disarray. Closets and armoire drawers spilled clothing. At the foot of the bed, a chest with a flowered paper interior had been emptied of everything but the ubiquitous white powder. The walls in the bedroom were painted a glossy ox-blood red. The real blood all over the floor was redder. The bed, front and center between two shaded street-facing windows, had a barred metal headboard and footboard. Miscellaneous objects were strewn across the bed's brown-striped sheets: an empty camera box, a bottle of Nic bug powder, an empty Verizon phone box, a paper bag, an encyclopedia, an empty vodka bottle, scissors, a roll of duct tape, a length of rope, a cylindrical black plastic container, a bottle of lube. On the floor were a bloodied cable box, a pile of folded white T-shirts, one stamped with a bloody shoe print, aspirin, snippets of rope, and scraps of black duct tape.

George was on his back in a pool of blood. He lay under the heap of a tan comforter which was partially blackened by blood and which must have slipped or been pulled from the bed. Only his duct-taped ankles and feet were visible. When the comforter was raised, George's face appeared covered with a dense scattering of white pills—aspirin. An aspirin bottle rested by his head.

George had been stabbed fifty times front and back. Some of these wounds were random cuts and slices, but the majority weren't. Both hands were injured in a messy way "consistent with" warding off a blade. From under his left ear to the area of his Adam's apple, there were four stabs and three incised wounds (wounds made by slicing). The carotid artery had been cut. The left temple had been stabbed, as well as the right cheek, a deep stab that penetrated George's cheek and tongue. There were also two incised wounds and a stab to the back of the head and one behind the right ear. The haphazard nature and changing angles of these injuries suggested to the ME that the victim was alive and struggling when they were made.

On the pale-as-flour skin of George's back, six stab wounds were grouped at his left shoulder and eleven on his right side below the scapula. These were up to two inches deep, and some went through his ribs to penetrate his chest cavity. The ME explained that clustered wounds like these are made when the victim is not (or no longer) moving. Seven more stab wounds formed a cluster in the middle of George's chest, including a deep one near his heart. Finally, six gaping incised wounds, roughly parallel, running down George's pale left arm, made it look like a ghastly version of an unbaked baguette.

George was wearing a black T-shirt which had been pushed up over his chest. His pants were unbuckled, un-buttoned, and unzipped. They were pulled down below his knees. So were his boxer shorts. The shaft of his penis was bruised from possible squeezing. An additional circu-lar area of bruising to the head of the penis was reportedly consistent with a bite.

While listening to this matter-of-fact, yet horrific, testi-mony, John leans back in his chair as usual, his legs flung out under the defense attorney's table. He appears buried in himself, buried by choice and as deeply as possible. He is uncannily motionless, his cheeks red from consciousness of the eyes that keep shifting toward him. The scene as described differs so much from a single accidental poke to the neck that left George still mumbling and cursing when John disappeared that night.

V. The Trial

Spiro and Beth Katehis, John's parents, were married after they'd known each other five days. Spiro, twenty-one, was about to fly back to Greece with his grandfather and already had a plane ticket. Beth, eighteen, was anxious to get away from her Dominican American family, so when Spiro told her the only way he could stay was if they got married, she agreed. John was born two years later. The marriage ended in bitterness three years after that.

Though never brought into evidence, John's school records show a very troubled kid. He wasn't in the public school system but attending a special school for the emotionally disturbed in Westchester County. He was suspended repeatedly. He harassed a girl for taking her medication. He exposed himself on the school bus and engaged in other "sexually inappropriate behavior." He threatened a teacher. He vengefully took one kid's backpack, threw it in a toilet, and peed on it. He got into fights. An eerie report in the file contains the observation that he "seems to enjoy the pain and discomfort of others." Also on file was something John himself wrote at twelve: "When I grow up I want to be a killer."

In 2000 Beth had a daughter, Bethany Angelica. Beth doted on the girl and sent her to the John Robert Powers school in New York City, a somewhat faded performing arts feeder for kids who want to get into TV commercials and movies.

Clips of nine-year-old Bethany Angelica's dances and "runway with poise and confidence" school performances were uploaded to YouTube by GODDESSBETH, but languished online with only a few adoring comments from

GODDDESSBETH herself, princessbeth0413, and sometimes, sweetly, greekjohn92.

Beth is short and large-busted. Her hair, sometimes mahogany, sometimes blondish, falls to her shoulders in loose strands doctored with a hair crimper. She dresses carefully, wears large sunglasses, and carries a clear vinyl bag. She has a taste for pearlescent fingernail and toenail polish and elaborate makeup including foundation and vaguely bluish sparkling lipstick with contrasting purplish lip liner. As "LadyBeth" she has posted several low-quality videos of herself dancing to a Lady Gaga song, for example, or doing a tame fake striptease to a Sinatra number with an umbrella as a prop. Sometimes Beth came to court with a heavyset white-bearded producer/director/handbag designer and Segway aficionado named Itsi Atkins, who believed a movie deal was in the air and wanted to be part of it.

Beth had a remote poise with reporters. Completely unprepared for media attention, her ex-husband Spiro seemed to have a much harder time being "public." A newspaper picture from the arraignment caught him sobbing, his balding, flyaway hair a mess, while an expressionless Beth stands next to him, her fingers just touching his tie, a stony gesture of comfort. Long afterward, Spiro still resented that picture. After it was taken he shaved his head, a much better look for him.

Spiro is also small. His fancy trial clothes usually looked too big on him. Nervous, he always came early, scuttling down the hall with a side-to-side gait, cell phone in hand like an old-fashioned bookie with his pad. He was working overnight shifts as a waiter in a Queens diner and got little sleep. During testimony his leg bounced constantly, his hands trembled. He sniffled at regular intervals and was often just shy of crying. Like an agonized sports fan, he sat forward on the blond-wood courtroom bench watching John's attorney spar with the judge. Unable to keep still or repress derisive snorts, he was reprimanded and almost asked to leave the courtroom twice.

Spiro and Beth have the personality differences, the sour hostility, that suggest the unwanted aftermath of an intense, youthful passion. But neither seems likely to have sired or raised a monster. She comes across as a little cool or self-involved, Spiro a little hot-headed.

More interesting, Spiro appears to be completely smitten with his son. He claims they were like brothers, and so they appear in MySpace pictures, both in black heavy metal T-shirts standing in front of a big Ozzy Osbourne logo. Strangely, looks apart, Spiro comes off as the younger, idolizing one. In court his love is naked and innocent, and he watches the proceedings with an expression of anguish.

(Boy and man are profoundly mixed up in this case. It isn't just that middle-aged George had a taste for kiddie cartoon lunch boxes, or that his fetish might have reproduced a childhood event, or that the child John Katehis's taste ran to swords and knives, or that he could admonish his elder by e-mail, "you've been a naughty boy"—father and son themselves seem reversed.)

At five-eleven, taller than either of his parents, bigger, handsomer, more poised, more adult-seeming, John was led to the defense table rear-handcuffed before every pretrial hearing in the spring and summer of 2010. Judge Neil Jon Firetog held these cattle calls on Fridays. Family members and lawyers crowded a fourth-floor courtroom as the judge summarily dispatched motions and scheduling matters for a slew of defendants, some of whom appeared by video-link from Riker's Island. The scene could get hectic as a sergeant expelled those who couldn't find seats; Firetog mocked a lawyer's Vivaldi-playing cell phone ("Either turn that off or change the ring tone"); a Chinese translator scrambled to a phone line open to the video booth at Riker's; and irrelevant but fascinating conversations were whispered nearly at one's ear: "My baby was shot in the back eight times." "Mm, that hurts." "They know it was a silver Audi, but they don't have a plate or a gun or a shooter."

John was often brought out late in the session when the crowd had thinned. Spiro and Beth and whoever had come with them might move to get a better spot for the brief moment when John would turn his head and hunt for them. He scanned others in the crowd as well, and sometimes, like a teenager—like most of the defendants—he'd play it tough.

From a distance his brown eyes look pure black. The bridge of his nose is broad, which gives him the tawny-skinned air of a lion in repose. A dent convinced anonymous "experts" online that his nose had been broken once. His long chin juts. He looks more like his mother than his nebbishy father, but outshines them both by far.

Brisk and unceremonious, anything but a showboater, Judge Firetog appeared to find the slick defense attorney, Jeffrey T. Schwartz, irritating from the start. A major flare-up occurred during a hearing on April 23. Schwartz appealed to have Weber's computer hard drive released. The computer likely did contain records of his exchanges with hustlers and maybe pornography, but Weber's reputation and past behavior really weren't at issue in this case (though of course they were). Firetog brusquely denied Schwartz's request because it had no relevance to the defense the lawyer was planning. "Why do you really want this information?"

Schwartz, wearing an overly white, overly even, but somehow confrontational smile, along with flashy cuff links, watch, and a quadruple-pointed handkerchief in the breast pocket of his chalk-stripe suit, replied, "Prosecution aims to prove Katehis came over to rob or attack Weber, but if we can establish Weber had a pattern of inviting over underage boys for sex . . ."

Firetog scooted forward. Shaking his robed forearm back and forth, he demanded, "But what is your defense?"

"It appears Weber invited our client, an underage boy, over—"

"It doesn't work that way. What is your defense?"

"It's been established that physical force is allowable in the case of an unwanted sexual assault."

"So this will be self-defense?" An outright argument of self-defense would be tough given the evidence.

"No," Schwartz conceded, but he continued arguing.

Firetog cut him off and explained with a great sigh that the computer information would be under seal and available as a possible appellate issue.

Still, Schwartz argued. He complained that the date Firetog set for the trial was too soon.

The trial began on October 18. Firetog's annoyance only increased. Schwartz was combative and scattershot before jury selection. He claimed he hadn't had enough time to prepare; police officers had failed to determine reasonable cause; Katehis was the victim of an adult predator;

evidence of some kind of illegal sexual contact simply had to be introduced.

Schwartz kept at it until Firetog shouted him down wearily, "You can't argue facts that are not in the record!" When Schwartz still wouldn't back down, the judge threatened him with contempt of court if anything like this happened in front of a jury. The lawyer would be fined $2,500 per offense.

The following day saw a long and contentious discussion at the bench. The main points of the bench conference were later repeated for the record: defense felt the warnings of contempt of court, the mention of fines, and the number of objections sustained all indicated that the judge was unduly hostile. Schwartz felt his ability to defend his client was compromised. In conference he'd asked the judge to recuse himself. Sighing, yet elaborately conciliatory, Firetog tried to brush aside the mess.

Schwartz stood up. "I've never had an experience in my life where I've been threatened with contempt." He said he was an ex-prosecutor and understood trials from both sides, but in this case his guiding light was the best interests of his client. He claimed the judge was "chilling" their defense. "You have made me feel like a marked target. You have frightened and terrified my client, a sixteen-year-old boy, and his family." He claimed that John, Beth, and Spiro had all lost confidence in the judge's fairness.

For the record, Schwartz went on, he wanted to tell a story. "You have overpersonalized this," he said. "We've had an experience in the past."

Schwartz recounted that he'd been assigned a prominent case a year or so earlier. "Though my client wanted me," another lawyer "bad-mouthed" him, and the judge on the case shut Schwartz out. Schwartz said he'd filed a grievance against the judge in question even though "Your Honor" recommended against it. Firetog had told him to let it go. "You offered to give me another high-profile case." (Schwartz gravitates to prominent cases; he was representing John Katehis pro bono but getting some press attention for his efforts.)

Judge Firetog listened to all this and wondered aloud how any of it could have prejudiced him against Schwartz. They argued a bit more, but Firetog soon announced, "The motion for recusal is denied."

Schwartz then asked if he could go *at once* to the current chief administrative judge to have a new judge assigned to the case. "I can't operate with a target on my chest. I feel muzzled." He said he was so uncomfortable that he'd asked an ethics attorney to sit in on the proceedings.

Nonetheless, the trial continued. Schwartz was often slapped down with "asked and answered" and "objection sustained" even in the presence of the jury. (Once, during ADA Fliedner's testimony, the jury was ordered to file out for a moment, and Firetog gave Schwartz a quick browbeating.)

The defense didn't have much going for them, but the well-prepared slickness of the prosecution witnesses, police witnesses especially, may have been causing a few juror doubts about whether proper procedure had been followed during the investigation—an idea Schwartz was, of course, trying to foster. Spiro clearly believed that information about the Middletown capture was being held back. On the stand, Normile and Fliedner smoothly described Spiro as invariably cooperative. It must have hurt. Spiro was beside himself, red-faced, glaring, tearful, as he listened to them. They were making it sound like he'd betrayed his son. "Did you notice they wouldn't look at me?" he later asked me with a flash of uncomprehending rage.

Outside the courtroom, Spiro said he couldn't wait to get on the stand to tell his side of the story. But he never got the chance. The defense presented no case, perfectly normal in a situation like this where you're better off not opening your side to awkward questioning. To me, Spiro claimed the police had burst into his place, threatened to shove a cell phone down his throat if he didn't give them what they wanted, and then drove him up to Middletown in handcuffs. He skipped over the telephone call actually setting his son up for capture. But he clearly believed he and John had been wronged.

Tension was rising. Spiro hissed about Itsi Atkins. "I don't know what Beth thinks she's doing with him. He's a fucking producer. If he tries to sit in my place again I'm going to fucking kick the shit out of him." With sublime disgust, he complained that a Greek reporter had even mistaken the much older Itsi for him, Spiridon, the father.

In the men's room, where the plumbing made the constant unnerving sound of a patient on a respirator, Itsi suavely accosted me after seeing me talk to Spiro. "You might want to be careful who you talk to . . . I'm just saying. There are two sides in this, and they don't always see eye to eye. Just so you know, Beth and I are in control of the real information. And we have John's full support and approval."

Spiro, meanwhile, had seen me give Beth an e-mail and telephone number. He complained, "When I saw you do that, I thought, *Oh shit, he's just gonna get her side of things.* Did you see that huge fight we had yesterday? No? Good."

No quick verdict came the day the jury was sent to confer. Schwartz bustled and grinned nervously. The slender, long-haired assistant district attorney, Anna-Sigga Nico-lazzi, sat lonelier than ever at the prosecution table. Every so often her skinny elbows rose and she'd grasp the chair's armrests as if about to rise with an objection. She merely shifted, but with odd precision. (She was, incidentally, enormously pregnant with a little girl. In the context of her controlled and graphic descriptions of the murder, the pregnancy was a bit disconcerting.)

Before lunch the jury sent out notes requesting to re-view testimony. Later, a note came out saying they were having trouble reaching a verdict. They weren't sure what constituted reasonable doubt. The judge had them file back into the courtroom and recited his definition for them.

At 4:48 the jury sent out a note saying they still hadn't come to a unanimous verdict. Firetog highlighted their use of the words "at this point." The next day the jurors watched John's video confession again. They had more testimony read back. They asked about reasonable doubt yet again. They said they were still struggling to reach a verdict. Eventually, the judge called them out (John as well) and read what's called the Allen charge—basically, *Go back in there and really try!* Experienced reporters said the Allen charge rarely worked and was usually a prelude to a mistrial.

The final day was veiled in tedium. Around noon the press filled the front row reserved for them. I could over-hear whispers from a bench conference. "You want to try it again real soon?" "November 3?"

John was brought out at twelve twenty. Judge Firetog announced that the jury had sent out another note saying they were deadlocked, and he declared a mistrial. After

that came a flurry of administrative announcements. As re-
tained but unpaid counsel, Schwartz said he might not be
able to handle the retrial. John was left alone at the defense
table while his lawyer and a colleague went to fetch boxes
of trial material from a back room.

Firetog: "So they'll go to the 18B panel for a new public
defender. Who's up? Maybe Herbert Moser. Another ADA
may be necessary as well, due to ⸱ . . ." He nodded toward
the pregnant ADA. November 3 was announced as the date
for reassignment.

"Oh, and can we revisit bail?" Schwartz asked, returning with his boxes.

"Maybe," the judge said. "Let's see what the split was.
If they want to tell us the split."

The jury was led in and the mistrial was announced.
Several jurors tried to communicate dissent by stiffly shaking their heads. The judge thanked them all and dismissed
them, saying, with a wintry smile, that he'd see them all
again in eight years. John couldn't resist a grin as the jurors filed out. He looked surprised, though Schwartz had
boasted to reporters back when the first jury note came
out, "We won!"

It was agreed the judge would speak to the jury first.
After that the lawyers could debrief them. Then reporters
would be able to question willing ex-jurors.

But after a few moments Judge Firetog hurried back
into the courtroom, his black robe flying. It was strange
to see him off the elevated bench, on a level with the lawyers and other mortals. He rested a hand on the court reporter's desk. He was wearing a somewhat sheepish but
giddy expression. He slicked his black hair. "Something
very strange just happened. The minute I went in there

the jury told me, 'If we could have just an hour longer we could reach a verdict.'"

Schwartz jumped up and started to argue coercion. "They've been dismissed!"

"I didn't say a word to them," Firetog countered, then climbed onto the bench.

Schwartz was outraged: "This is unconscionable!"

The reporters scribbled in their steno pads.

Asked to respond to Schwartz, even Nicolazzi seemed at a loss. "Well, this is a very unusual situation, but . . ." It was obvious to everyone which direction the verdict had to be leaning.

Firetog hustled things along: "Let's bring out the defendant." John was brought back in looking deeply confused and, frankly, scared. As soon as he was uncuffed and the court officers had taken their usual seats behind him, Schwartz stood and argued for all he was worth.

The judge was adamant about pushing ahead. It was a rare opportunity, and it was worth trying to get a verdict from *this* jury.

"There *is* no jury. The jury's been dismissed."

Firetog announced, "The mistrial is vacated."

Schwartz kept arguing, until another note was passed to the judge, who quieted the defense lawyer with a wave of his hand. He said it now looked like all arguments were moot, because the jury was asking to speak to the lawyers. Firetog said this with an air of deflation, as if he thought he'd witnessed something magical—magical justice—only to realize at the last moment it was a clever fraud. The world worked in the same old messy and unjust way. The mistrial was reinstated.

"No backsies this time, judge?" Schwartz demanded.

It turned out the jury had taken three votes. The first was nine-to-three to convict. Three women voted to acquit. (Because he was young, cute? *No*, said juror seven, a man. Was it about the sex thing? *Tough at first, but we got over it.*) The second poll was ten-to-two. The final tally, eleven-to-one. The one woman held out, it was revealed, because she couldn't resolve a doubt about John's intent.

VI. *Time*

After almost a year, during a stretch of heartbreakingly golden late-fall weather in November 2011, John Katehis was tried again in Brooklyn Supreme Court. He was eighteen now and had been moved from the Robert N. Davoren Complex (detained male adolescents) to the Otis Bantum Correctional Center (detained male adults), both on Riker's Island. An eleventh grader when he went in, he'd passed his GED while imprisoned (with very high scores, Spiro insisted to me proudly). There'd also been a serious fight and a stretch in isolation.

On court days John would pull his pink shirt or his brown-striped one from under his cell mattress where he kept them "pressed." He'd wear one of these and a tan striped tie. By the end they were looking quite wrinkled. A beat-up white bus with grated windows swept him into the underground garage of the court building. The old cast of characters had assembled, along with a canny new defense lawyer, Jay Cohen, who hammered away at the unsavory sex details. But nearly a year had passed, and things were inevitably different the second time around. Judge Firetog conducted the trial with a slight air of haste. Prosecution seemed almost rote at first. Beth was absent sometimes, notably when the lawyers made summations and the day we waited for a verdict. One morning after stiffly scanning the crowd, John muttered almost inaudibly to himself, "Where is she?"

Spiro was obviously exhausted. (He was out of work and complained that he didn't have enough money for lunch one day.) I once noticed him asleep in his oversized pinstriped suit on a bench outside the courtroom. Later he fell asleep in the courtroom itself as a series of gruesome photographs was introduced into evidence—a bad moment for John. John turned to see his father's chin slumped on his chest and made a sour expression, undoubtedly feeling terribly alone.

Along with the sense of hurry came a sort of callused energy. Much more horrible photographs were introduced this time. The language was more graphic. Defense was more aggressive about disparaging George Weber's behavior. We even saw a shocking picture of the bruised (bitten?) penis. As the actual murder receded into the past, memory seemed to grow colder, more brutal. "I just need five more minutes, judge," Nicolazzi snapped at Firetog before her summation. Then she delivered her speech with stiff passion.

Though this time they were given the option of a second, lesser charge—manslaughter—the jury was slow again. Perhaps they couldn't forgive Weber's strange sexuality. Or they couldn't bear throwing a young man's life away. You could see the strain on jurors' ashen faces and imagine their weariness. They chose murder in the second degree, finally, the more serious charge (and the highest possible in New York, where first degree murder has to involve "special circumstances," like a police officer victim, multiple murders, or torture).

They'd decided John meant to kill. Until the foreman spoke the atmosphere had been heavy. Now Spiro looked faint, cameras chittered like squirrels, glances collided and retreated in the courtroom's suddenly frictionless air. John's mild self-confident expression froze. Poked on the shoulder by a court officer, he turned to give his father a big those-are-the-breaks smile and a shrug. A tough guy.

9
DESTRUCTION

It feels almost apocalyptic to end with a killing so pure. A relative speaking for Weber's family at the sentencing told John Katehis that the only motive he could imagine was that "you killed him because you could." He said the family believed it would have been somebody else if not Weber. Katehis's father sobbed, entirely alone, until his ex-wife hurried in halfway through the sentencing, her hair freshly blond and ironed flat. (Afterward I saw her—tiny, pert, solitary—on a subway platform; we pretended not to know one another and boarded a train several cars apart.)

When Weber's relative finished reading the victim impact statement, Judge Firetog dispensed with any stagey ruminations of his own and imposed the maximum sentence, saying "Twenty-five to life" so abruptly that a grin like a pulsing vein appeared on John's face.

In the elevator I asked two photographers who'd been sitting in the jury box and had a better view, "Was that some kind of nervous, uncontrolled laughing?"

One of the photographers shook his head and said, "That kid is always smiling. He always smiles except when the jury's around."

The sentencing smile was bigger than the "guilty" smile, but both were like catnip to morally minded reporters. After the "guilty" smile, one asked Katehis's father about "that big toothy grin" (not really what it was), and Spiro pleaded, "He was just nervous. That's the way he is." Both smiles looked like nerves to me too, the nerves of someone who, like many young men, has traded away emotion for dignity.

Katehis's smiles were, in a sense, smiles at his own destruction. As a kid I learned to smile ironically too, when I was in trouble in public or when someone pressed me to feel something I refused to feel. The scale of Katehis's trouble and irony boggle the mind, however, and his remoteness from what he did must be just as vast.

It went far beyond a hate crime. Perhaps Katehis had been abused, as a friend furiously claimed (shouting further, "Weber's the real criminal, and I'll tell you, he's fucking burning in hell!"). Or Katehis had particular spite for gay men. Or, paradoxically, he felt a scornful confidence, or even a sense of comfort, around them. The point seems to have been to find a disposable human being who was willing to "be weak," to be the ultimate "bottom," someone whom people wouldn't trouble about later. The point was the act of violence itself.

If this is true, then Katehis may represent what I've been looking for in this book at its most radical or uninflected: pure masculinity enraged. It isn't an inconsequential thing that he stared me down halfway through the first trial. He must have been sick of my gaze, of being watched constantly by a stranger, of being "mugged." Overpowering me with black-eyed menace must have been satisfying. He's obviously profoundly troubled, but I see a twisted manliness in him rather than insanity, which is ultimately as guiltless as a storm or a landslide.

In this case, there was a particular if incomprehensible

choice to kill. The story shrinks to its synopsis, a brute ex-
hibition of youth and strength and domination and power.
At this point my work—this book—becomes something
like staring into John's eyes: either I've arrived at a dimen-
sionless point of darkness at the heart of violence, or the
labor of looking so intently has become a sort of faintness.

I'm aware that calling John Katehis's crime an "Honor
Hilling" is wrong. Not just because I believe that true
honor—whatever else it is—can never be associated with
a murder, but also because the case appears to fall into another well-known category, the thrill killing, perhaps the
most disturbing type of crime. Strangely, it's also the most
natural murder, in the sense that it's the most animal. It
is motiveless murder for its own sake, murder as play or
as experience. Someone who spoke extensively with John
after the crime was asked by a reporter what the motive
could have been and answered, "Some people are just
evil." Given the outcome, it's a moot point (for everyone
except John and anybody who loves him or wants to help
him) whether this was a case of real evil or its youthful imi-
tation. Whether John is a soulless tough guy or was merely
acting like one doesn't matter.

Earlier, I wrote about the joy of violence. Though by
itself thrill or pleasure rarely suffices as a motive for murder, it can be glimpsed often in this book. A wild physical pleasure of release—the sense of not being present that
Steve Mullins and Juan Flythe described—may account for
the barbarity of some of the crimes. Parrish's fifty wounds,
Weber's fifty. Billy Jack's crushed head and burned body.
Darrell Madden, however studied his craziness may have
been in the beginning, eventually developed a taste for violence, a connoisseurship even. I heard admiration in his

description of Bradley Qualls's frenzy. Even Ben Williams appears to have gloried in his naked attack on Timothy Renault. These look like experiences of an (ironically) sexlike transcendence. Even if self-consciousness at the animal moment of attack is impossible, it's likely that anticipation of or satisfaction in the act felt, for a few seconds at least, like brute and happy manliness to the killers.

I haven't been trying prove a thesis by recounting these stories. If anything, I've wanted to make thinking about them more complex, more tentative. It's been my special concern to point out differences. Still, something fundamental about John Katehis's crime leads me back to the beginning to reconsider how the *acte gratuit*, the simple, pointless murder, was elaborated in the minds of other murderers by ideas like honor and purity or by emotions like hatred and pride.

I began by looking at murders by young men where a sexual element, either real or metaphorical, entered the equation. The typical victim has been a gay man, but as I've said repeatedly, "hate crimes" and "gay panic murders"—indeed all limiting labels, including "honor killings"—strike me as insufficient. Certain types of murderers seem to gravitate toward certain types of victims. Men who kill women or female prostitutes, though hatred is often involved, aren't usually called hate criminals. Men who kill their wives aren't motivated by ideology, though sexuality is probably a factor. The men who kill gay men are equally diverse, and their motives also have layers of complexity.

A complication of the basic, Katehis-like act of murder is clear in Jonathan Schmitz's confession to the 911 operator in Michigan. "He picked on me on national TV. He fucked me." Jon used an explicit sexual metaphor without thinking. It isn't by chance that the verb "dishonor" was once used euphemistically to describe a woman's rape. However misguided, Schmitz was feeling an explosive agony of dishonor at the time of the killing. The other key words he used were "national TV." Honor is a public phenomenon.

In one way or another, almost all these killings involved supersensitivity to public appearance. Steven Parrish was murdered for that reason alone. The decision was made in such frankly foolish haste that it's obvious how urgent—burning—an issue image must have been for the members of his gang. But even Steve Mullins now says he turned a purely personal "affront" into a public issue by telling "a lot" of people that he planned to kill Billy Jack Gaither. Since he mentions friends suggesting that he merely beat Gaither up, the way he told people must have resembled a consultation. This is how honor is dealt with. It's a community matter. In the old days of duels, there were seconds, days of advice and consideration, accepted routines, even handbooks. Darrell Madden was so adept at deception and performance that he probably had little sense where to draw the line between private and public in his own life. Yet he says he allowed violence to escalate since "I couldn't say anything about him hitting [Mr. Domer] because of how it would have made me look." It doesn't sound like he was worried specifically about being found out to be homosexual. Some broader concern about appearance was involved.

A high level of rationalization shows up in many of the cases. Madden spoke of murder as a "mission" and, however dishonestly, he participated in a gang with ranks and rules. His murderous mission was to oversee a ritual display of loyalty. This was a kind of coming out ceremony for Bradley Qualls. Benjamin Matthew Williams refers in passing to a similar ritual of "showing heart," but when it came to murder, his own rationalizations went far beyond gang loyalty. He built or inherited an entire ideology, albeit incoherent, which offered an intellectual (as opposed to an emotional) foundation for assassination and fire-bombing. All cool dutifulness, Steven Parrish's killers rigidly insisted they did what had to be done. Even Steve Mullins reached for a higher rationalization after avenging his personal honor. Granting that what he did had been wrong, he told Connie Chung that God had forgiven him, but Billy Jack was in hell, because that's what the Bible says. (And it does.) I doubt he truly holds to that article of faith. Even at the time, his claim may have been a defensive, public show of religiosity stiffened by Chung's aggression. The point is, thinking is involved far more than panic.

Hatred was a critical factor in these murders. It would be poisonous to pretend otherwise. If Schmitz or the 92 Family Swans thought it was so great a dishonor to be perceived as "gay," they must have accepted as truth that being gay is contemptible. Darrell Madden's entire life was deformed by that conviction. But even hatred is more complex than we like to think. Perhaps Steve Mullins wouldn't have felt affronted if a woman asked to give him a blow job, but he still may have scorned her. And even if he'd accepted, he may have felt contempt. The murder he first dreamed of had "a minority" as a victim. Though he used that word to mean a black man, it's still illuminating. In a sense, "a minority," any minority, is what he was looking for. As a young man with a certain charisma, it's no surprise that he eventually came upon a gay man. Similarly, Ben Williams's hatred had a broad spectrum. He had plenty to spare for Jews, black people, Mormons. People concerned about "hate crimes" sometimes dream that universal education about our differences will make intolerance vanish. Certainly, familiarity helps a lot. But in these cases, hatred often seems to exist *prior* to its having a clear object. Not only that, but Steve Mullins's exclusive sexual experiences with African Americans remind us that racist revulsion may differ by a hair's breadth from desire. Sex as fascination can trump both love and hatred. Violence is apparently similar.

If hatred can come before hating, murder can come before killing. Here I want to go beyond honor, hatred, thrill, to touch on psychopathy and derangement. The passenger who just misses an airplane that later crashes often claims to have had a weird feeling about the flight beforehand. A premonition like that is based on fallacy. Air travel is infrequent and dramatic enough that nearly every flier before nearly every flight thinks at least in passing about the possibility of disaster. The idea that any of these murders could have been predicted should be treated with caution. Still, every twelve-year-old doesn't say, *When I grow up I want to be a killer*. It doesn't lessen their guilt to say there's something wrong with many murderers. Troubling hints of violence were common during the childhood of John Katehis. Mullins's murder was, as he described it to me, secretly preexistent. Darrell Madden had a long history of violence and perhaps murder. Even the mild-mannered time bomb Jonathan Schmitz, someone who hadn't had the brutalizing experience of prison like Mullins and Madden, had toyed with self-murder. A disaffected Benjamin Matthew Williams proposed assassinating the leaders of the Living Faith Fellowship long before he committed any known crime.

Though I think all the killers I've written about have been disturbed to some extent, and though murders are, in fact, rare, these crimes are exemplary (in a purely negative sense) social acts, so they speak to us about the everyday world, or they at least make us reflect. My own slant hasn't been sociological. I don't offer a proposal to do anything about it all. This isn't a political work. My purpose has been descriptive—compiling a sort of list—and since my descriptions are pitched at the level of the individual, I haven't been able to avoid communicating a tragic sense of life. That doesn't always sit well with the proud or the confident or the optimistic or the cheerful: Americans. The "book of life" is by tradition a list, not so different from a catalog of ships or the index of a natural history field guide or the sequence of nucleotides in a genome. Gigantic lists have a gorgeous abundance often rejected for the sake of a summary or a concise position. But lists, by their very *list*ness, actually do make a quiet argument—inclusive, accepting, weary, a little sad like the farmer plowing furrows or the writer writing lines—about their contents, an argument against the destruction or loss of a single detail.

Acknowledgments

People from every part of the country and every imaginable walk of life have generously offered their time, their memories, and their reflections to help with this book. They've talked, written, thought hard, shown me places, shown me photographs. In no particular order I want to thank those I relied on most: Detective Gary Childs, Detective Joseph Caskey, Mort and Linda Domer, Spiro Katehis, Michelle Hensley, Jeff and Ann Monroe, McGregor Scott, an important informant who asked to remain anonymous, Joshua Lyon, Floyd Martin, John Maringouin, Steve Mullins, Darrell Lynn Madden, and Paul Gordon Smith Jr.

An even greater number of people took the time to offer or clear up details, correct my confusions—explain how a certain gun works, for example, or describe a legal strategy. Again in no particular order, I express my appreciation to: Mark McLaurin, Eric Rubio, Karney Hatch, Nathan McConnell, Randy O'Quinn, criminal investigator Rick Batt, Jay Cohen, Susan Domer, Assistant DA Anna-Sigga Nicolazzi, Daniel Goldin, Hamilton Nolan, Frank Morano, "Damian Hospital," and Jonah Bruno of the Brooklyn DA's press office.

Journalists were particularly open and helpful to someone who isn't really a fellow journalist at all. Thanks to Sam Stanton of the *Sacramento Bee*, Marcus Franklin of the Associated Press, William Gorta of the *New York Post*, William Sherman of the *New York Daily News*, Joseph Fenity, Simon Garron-Caine, and, most important of all, Duncan Osborne of *Gay City News*.

In addition to volumes of court records, the news outlets and websites I relied on are far too numerous to mention. Key information, however, came from the *Sacramento Bee*, ABC News *20/20*, PBS *Frontline*, the *New York Times*, the *Los Angeles Times*, the *Advocate*, the *Oklahoman*, the *Daily Ardmoreite*, *Slate*, *Gawker*, unfinishedlivesblog.com, lgbthatecrimes.org, georgeweberthenewsguy. blogspot.com, adl.org, mansonfamilypicnic.com, sallywilliams. org (defunct), whitereference.blogspot.com, YouTube.com, Wikipedia.org, findadeath.com, newsok.com, and maps.google. com. I'm responsible for any factual errors in the book.

I relied on the literary comments and advice of more people than I can remember who read part or all of the manuscript in one state or another, often rough. Special thanks to Patrick Ryan, Bob Smith, Keith McDermott, Vestal McIntyre, Bob Glück, Edmund White, David Ebershoff, Lisa Howorth, Claire Howorth, and Edward Orloff. Some just lent an ear and encouragement or did me a favor along the way, including Angelo Nikolopoulos, Matthew Goldin, Theresa Starkey, Susan Turner, Michael Carroll, Nora Wright, Justin Spring, Evan Wright, Zachary Lazar, Jim Holt, Jon McMillan, Bruce Benderson, Jerl Surratt, Rick Whitaker, Chris Bram, Giovanni Lucchetti, Dale Peck, Everett McCourt, Ken Siman, Steven Baker, Kevin Pinzone, Jeff Bond, Michael Slipp, Peter Cameron, Richard Kaye, Sam Roche, Stephen Bottum, Matthias Leutrum, and Thomas Keith.

I owe a unique debt to Don Weise, publisher of Magnus Books. We were at a bar together when I jokingly invented a "big-selling" true crime book for him—*Gay Panic: Men Who Kill the Men Who Love Them*. The harsh joke was the ultimate forebear of what became a serious passion of mine. Zachary Pace is responsible for finding a place for this book when it had none; his enthusiasm always bolstered me. Johnny Temple has made it a better book than it was, despite my occasional heel-dragging. Ibrahim Ahmad and Johanna Ingalls of Akashic Books have been indispensible, as have my agent, Monique DiDonna, and Sarah Russo, my publicist.

"Thanks" are probably out of order, but I want to at least acknowledge the people who chose not to talk to me, whether from pain, mistrust, or just emotion-charged dilatoriness. If you come across the book, I hope you see I did everything I could to make it fair. By far the most important of those who didn't talk to me are the ones who couldn't, the ones who really had no choice at all about being in this book. I especially hope I've honored them, not with a eulogistic black veil, but with bright light and a compassionate awareness of our shared humanity.

Finally, for me everything begins and ends with Darrell Crawford.